HOW TO
MAKE MONEY HOMESTEADING

So You Can Enjoy a Secure, Self-Sufficient Life

WITH 18 INSPIRATIONAL REAL-LIFE PROFILES

by
Tim Young

Copyright

Table of Contents

Introduction

"Instead of wondering when your next vacation is, maybe
you should set up a life you don't need to escape from."
— Seth Godin

Money. It is surprising that something so central to our way
of life is not often listed as one of the first words young
children learn. Make no mistake, though: toddlers learn of money's
importance more quickly than they learn the word itself, as they
watch mommy and daddy plunk down cash (if they are old
fashioned) to buy girl scout cookies, piano lessons, and cotton candy
at the fair, or use credit cards and, increasingly, digital currencies
to purchase groceries, clothes, toys, and virtually everything else.
To a child's eyes, it may appear that nothing is more basic, more
necessary to the human experience than money.

But what is money anyway? When you strip away all the mumbo
jumbo of complex financial talk, you realize money is nothing more
than a claim on human effort—simple as that. You work, someone
pays you (claiming the output of your work) with a monetary
instrument (such as dollars) and you are free to use those dollars
to purchase whatever you want or need. Of course, whatever you
purchase was produced with someone else's effort, so by making
the purchase, you are in effect purchasing (or claiming) someone
else's effort.

Unlike our distant ancestors for whom money was either
nonexistent or, at most, trivial to their lives, we were born into a
world where money and labor have woven an intricate web that

surrounds us, traps us, and, far too often, virtually suffocates us with debt.

If you doubt this, consider how many times you have thought about money. How to make more <u>money</u>, how to <u>pay</u> bills, how to <u>fund</u> your retirement, what you can <u>afford</u>, what you must <u>forgo</u>, how to <u>pay</u> for a trip or vacation, <u>pay</u> for education, <u>afford</u> the cost of health care or prescriptions, <u>pay</u> off the mortgage, whether a job <u>pays</u> enough, and so on. If you think that being independently wealthy would mean you would never have to worry about money again, perish that thought, for even the wealthy fret over paying taxes. In fact, according to a study by Prince & Associates, while fewer than 20 percent of Americans with less than $1 million worry about being sued, over 80 percent of people worth $20 million or more worry about being the target of a lawsuit. So money does not discriminate when casting its fretful spell as it retains a firm grasp over most people's lives, rich, poor, or middle class.

What is the hypnotic power of money anyway? And why do we always seem to want more of it?

I suspect what we really want is not money. Rather, we simply desire increased freedom…the ability to do more of what we want, when we want, without our time (labor) being controlled by someone else. And since most of us were born into a world centered on money, we seem to believe the path to this increased freedom is having more of it.

But is there another way?

In the first chapter, you will see that the largest categorical expenses for most people are, in order, housing, transportation, and food. Shelter and food have always been essential for human survival, of course, but why transportation? Because to survive in our modern world, families must travel to and from one or more jobs daily. This dictates automobile purchases or loan payments, insurance payments, repair costs, and most of all, weekly fuel purchases.

Now ask yourself this: What if this "status quo" were not the case? Rather than simply <u>consuming</u>, what if a family began to <u>produce</u> most of what they spend their income on today and worked for no one other than themselves? Could they not achieve the increased freedom (and happiness) they long for?

As you ponder this question, let me ask you to consider a few others:

- How fulfilling is your current lifestyle? Your job, where you live, how you spend your time… are you living your life or someone else's?

- Are you becoming more or less confident about your government's fiscal management policies, its ability to fund the entitlement programs it has committed itself to, balance the budget and service the ever-expanding national debt?

- Are you pleased with the nutritional quality and safety of the food your family consumes? Are you happy to consume a diet of food that is increasingly derived from genetically modified organisms (GMOs) and, unless you eat organic, doused with chemicals?

- If you have children, are they connected to the real (natural) world? Do they spend much of their time in nature, observing and being a part of natural life as children have done for millennia? Or are they trapped within the web of mankind's creation, heads down, hypnotized by a 4.3-inch digital display?

- If you enjoy eating meat, do you think industrial farm animals are treated fairly before they arrive neatly packaged in your refrigerator? Is that the meat you want to feed your family?

- Do you possess the most basic survival skills that our ancestors knew firsthand, such as how to grow and preserve food, how to raise and, if necessary, butcher animals or how to sew, and make your own soaps and medicines?

- Are you secure with your sources of income and are you confident they will continue?

If the answer to any of these questions is no—and for many (if not most) people it is—then you may feel you are being tugged by an ancient calling. Perhaps you hear the voice calling softly… a subliminal whisper. Or, it could be screaming to you that something has changed, shouting that something is wrong. This voice promises you an easier life, a simpler, more grounded life void of complexity and full of wonder.

It is calling you away from your life of voluntary complexity toward a life of voluntary simplicity.

MODERN HOMESTEADING

The idea of homesteading is not a new one. As a species, we humans seemingly mastered the art of living off the land, learning along the way to capture fire, clothe ourselves, and even preserve the food we learned to grow so it could later nourish us. These were remarkable advancements, but we were not content to stop there.

Mankind continually "evolved" to abandon hunting skills, opting instead to crowd tens of thousands of animals into small yards and houses, dose the animals' feed with antibiotics so they would live long enough to reach slaughter weight, and ignore the muted cries from concerned consumers that we were polluting our soil and water, creating deplorable working conditions while nurturing favorable conditions for pathogens such as e.coli 0157H7, salmonella, and listeria monocytogenes. Pathogens that, in a subterfuge that rivals the Trojan Horse, seek to kill us after we ingest them.

Although the modern age has given rise to many conveniences, technologies, and possibilities, many of us are wondering if we have gone too far. Yet, despite the preceding paragraphs, this is a book filled with hope for you and your family, not with despair.

As a species, we now find ourselves barely able to live on our own in the natural world, having accumulated too many allergies, too many dependencies on modern conveniences, too heavy a reliance on government assistance and, not that the mirror will let us forget, too many excess pounds to make it in the "real" world. For a growing number of us who recognize and are disturbed by this, the reassuring voice of Mother Nature is calling her children home to a simpler life.

For some, the call to self-sufficiency can be viewed as extreme and is taken very literally. These folks are inclined to head deep into the woods, make a cabin out of earthen materials, and learn to fend for themselves. They need no money and as far as the rest of us are concerned, they are out of sight, out of mind. In fact, some reality television shows feature people like these, most notably in Alaska. Ironically, these people's desire to be so isolated and independent from society made them such a novelty to us all that we "civilized" beings invaded their world with camera crews, thereby sabotaging their dreams of seclusion.

However, I believe this is not what most people want when they contemplate homesteading. Rather, they seek to become "modern homesteaders."

Modern homesteaders look for a compromise between the conveniences of contemporary life and the independence of traditional life; for a way to blend the two together to live in society yet be as self-sufficient as they desire.

This book aims to reach those of you who aspire to be modern homesteaders. Those who long to get closer to nature and increase your self-sufficiency and personal security by living more independently "off the land." Who daydream simply of growing your own food, cooking meals from scratch and not caring what day it is, but rather, understanding what season it is and what foods are in season. For meat eaters, this includes the hope of raising your own livestock with love and respect and perhaps learning to hunt wild game and butcher the meat yourself before placing it on the grill or, better yet, pressure canning the meat to last for years. Who knows? Maybe you are hoping to save the feathers and pelts, tan the hides and take pride in making leather, crafts, jewelry, or your own clothes.

Yet modern homesteaders like these prefer to not travel back to life of the early 1800s. While society is functioning as "it" is today, they would like access to local hospitals, though they hope their new lifestyle and diet will mean medical attention is rarely, if ever, needed. Still, they sleep better knowing that "it" is there.

Similarly, modern homesteaders may enjoy entertainment such as sports, concerts, movies or even watching Alaskan homesteaders on television, but they do not want it to be necessary. Often, those new to homesteading, the way my wife and I were eight years ago, *think* they will want these distractions, only to find the call from suburbia growing fainter each year as they become one with the land, at peace and at home. Let the natural world be your entertainment. Let the landscape be your gym.

While the Alaskan homesteaders featured on reality television may not be aware of the Internet, most people are and they know the information genie is out of the bottle. It is hard to imagine living without a resource so valuable to so many people around the globe, a resource that did not exist a mere generation ago. They may be able to kick the habit of frivolous social media sites but they know the Internet can inform them and teach them many skills, including the homesteading skills they so long to learn. They also know the Internet can be a tool to provide income to help them achieve their homesteading dreams. So as long as times are good and the grid is up, modern homesteaders want access to this tool, a tool that must be paid for. With money.

What modern homesteaders want is increased independence, autonomy, freedom… whatever you want to call it. They want to enjoy life, to eat as much nutritious and flavorful food off the land as possible and live as they see fit, but, if they get an itch, may choose to indulge at a fine restaurant. They (we) do not see themselves as weirdos and do not want to be weirdos. Rather, they recognize the dangers of the absurdly perilous world that we have collectively created and are looking for an escape route—a Plan B.

They desire to opt out of depending on modern society but do not necessarily want to be excluded from this society. In short, modern homesteaders do not aspire to retreat deep into the Alaskan wilderness, never to be heard from again.

PAYING THE BILLS

So, with such an increasing number of people attracted to the idea of leaving their homeowner's associations (HOA) behind, why are more people not ditching their cubicles and heading in droves back to the land?

The answer - MONEY.

Money… the human invention that does not exist for any other species, the instrument we created to trade labor for "stuff." A monetary instrument now so ubiquitously necessary, we cannot even aspire to live meagerly without it on a piece of land owned free and clear. After all, the tax man cometh.

Modern homesteading is alluring to many but we still must pay taxes, need to purchase fuel, and most of us desire health care in catastrophes. The thought of walking away from our current lives and jobs leaves us shaking in our boots when we realize the burden of earning money with no weekly paycheck to fall back on falls squarely on our shoulders. At least that is the case for full-time homesteaders.

Alas, we find that the first step of transitioning from a life of consumption to a life of production begins with figuring out how to produce our own income.

For almost everyone (other than serial entrepreneurs) this is a new and scary realization. After all, we were born into a society that conditioned us to seek employment, gave us job descriptions with rigid schedules such as "work from eight to five, Monday to Friday," but allowed us to have weekends (another unnatural creation of mankind) off. And to take a few weeks off each year for vacation.

It may genuinely surprise people immersed in that world to learn that nature has no such schedule, no such rules. Cows calve on Christmas and birthdays, gardens must be harvested on weekends—football or not. As a new and modern homesteader, you will get to (in fact, have to) create your own job description and set your own priorities with the goal of earning sufficient income to afford you the lifestyle you want off the land.

In other words, ironically, your first step as a modern homesteader is to think like an entrepreneur. Since you will be doing it off the land, I encourage you to think of yourself as an agripreneur!

WHO THIS BOOK IS FOR

This book is for anyone interested in finding ways to live more self-sufficiently. And remember, self-sufficiency includes financial self-sufficiency. From this point of view, the book's goal is to get you thinking about how you can generate income while embracing a more self-sufficient lifestyle. For some readers that will mean a large acreage with farm income as a component. Other readers may be tied to a city apartment but are looking for ideas to develop portable income streams they can take with them once they are able to commit to full-time homesteading. Still other readers may be more interested in saving money than in generating income. They may worry about feeding a family of four for less than a couple of hundred dollars a month. Others still may be nearing retirement with the promise of a modest pension or social security, yet feel the urge to opt out of suburbia to embrace a more self-sufficient lifestyle. If any of these resonate with you, then this book with its profiles of people who have succeeded in doing exactly these things will surely help and inspire you.

I use several phrases in this book to describe people who generate income while embracing self-sufficient lifestyles. In some cases, you will see the phrase "homesteader" while in others, you may read "farmsteader." These are essentially the same, with the only difference perhaps being the latter implies having land and offering more traditional farming products. I also use self-sufficient, prepper, preparedness, self-reliance and other phrases that all refer to living a similar lifestyle.

FEATURED CASE STUDY PROFILES

To give the reader as broad and realistic expectations as possible regarding what farmstead models are possible, I include profiles of 18 different farmstead individuals and/or families. Each have been generous with their time and answers and I believe you will benefit tremendously from their knowledge. By reading their answers carefully, you will gain valuable insight into what works as well as what does not—at least for some folks. You will read what they believe they did right as well as what they would do differently if they could do it all over again.

Prior to conducting these brief interviews, I did not know most of the interviewees. Indeed, although I have met some and know a couple reasonably well, I still have not met most of those profiled. Therefore, this group was selected not because they were among my personal acquaintances, but rather because I researched and sought examples from various geographic locations of people who had implemented diverse homestead enterprises. Some are authors and full-time bloggers, others are tinkerers and micro-entrepreneurs while others still rely on more traditional farming enterprises for income. What they share in common is a passion for self-sufficiency. And, they almost all have embraced the concept of multiple streams of income.

I am grateful to each of them for their contributions. I hope you benefit from their experiences and the stories they shared inform and inspire you. If that happens, I have included names of their websites, books and blogs so that you can find out more about them. Perhaps you may even try to reach out to them. After all, they too were in your shoes!

WHAT THIS BOOK IS

This book is designed to *introduce* you to the numerous ways you can earn money from becoming more self-sufficient. It does not tell you what to to. Rather it is a *tool* to help you to develop your own income-generation plan so you can make the transition from traffic to tractor, from cubicle to cabin. It is organized as follows:

- Chapter One describes steps to consider BEFORE you begin homesteading.
- Chapter Two provides ideas to Make Money With Your Land.
- Chapter Three focuses on how to Make Money With Your Skills.
- Chapter Four shares ways to Make Money With your Farmstead Products.
- Chapter Five reveals ways to Save Money by Homesteading (which reduces the need to earn money).

- Chapter Six shows you how to Personalize Your Farmstead Business Plan.
- Chapter Seven helps you put the pieces together for Self-Sufficient Income, including looking at homesteading as a retirement plan.

Many ideas listed in these chapters are presented in great detail. Others are simply listed because they are intuitively obvious. The book's aim is to give you ideas rather than comprehensive knowledge, and to let you determine which path you are interested in and want to explore further.

How to Make Money Homesteading also assumes you have an interest in becoming more self-sufficient and that you are interested in ideas on how to make money as a homesteader, a farmer or both. This book provides many excellent ideas for earning anywhere from a modest to very comfortable income and shares numerous case study profiles of others who have already successfully done just that.

As a farmer and homesteader myself, I have personal experience with many of the ideas presented in this book—if not most. While this book draws partially from my own experience, it includes 18 profiles of others who have made a life of homesteading or farming, at least to some degree, and shares with you how they achieved their goals.

WHAT THIS BOOK IS NOT

Of course, while this book is detailed and specific in many ways, it must be viewed as a *starting point* for each individual reader. With so many specifics unique to each reader, such as level of debt, skills, cash, health, knowledge and countless other factors, *How to Make Money Homesteading* does not aim to inform each reader of exactly how to homestead. There are countless books on homesteading skills, though few (if any) present actionable ideas on how to make money on the homestead. <u>That is what this book is all about</u>. It is designed to get you, the reader, thinking about what you want, what you are capable of and shows many of the possible ways you can earn income while pursuing a more self-sufficient lifestyle.

The good news is this: There are TONS of ways to generate dependable, steady income in rural America! This book lists dozens of them, but these represent just the tip of the iceberg. Viewed all at once, it may seem overwhelming and dangerous, making you think it might be best to just stay put in the safety of your cubicle. However, as Winston Churchill said:

"The optimist sees opportunity in every danger; the pessimist sees danger in every opportunity."

I hope that like me, you are an optimist!

So are you ready? Excellent! Prepare to get back to your roots and join the growing legion of recovering consumers!

Chapter One
Preparing to Homestead

"So many fail because they don't get started—they don't go. They don't overcome inertia. They don't begin."

— Ben Stein

"Can you make a living as a farmer, prepper or homesteader?" I have been asked this question countless times in person or via email. The answer is YES, but this often comes with a caveat: Each person has to rethink what "a living" is. You may currently lead a typical American lifestyle, but that does not mean that is the life you wish to lead. After all, if it is, then why are you interested in becoming more self-sufficient?

The *typical* American household can be considered a weapon of mass consumption. It CONSUMES food, energy, clothing, entertainment, education, and more FROM the American economy. That is by design, of course, and contributes to the very real sense of indebtedness that so many feel.

By contrast, the *ideal* American homestead is centered on production. It PRODUCES food, alternative energy, clothing, entertainment, education, and more FOR the American economy. The items a homestead produces can serve to meet its own needs, be sold for cash or be used for trade and barter. These are all ways the homestead divorces itself to a large degree from fiat currency and creates its own form of self-sufficient currency. If money is needed to pay taxes, the homestead can sell items or services that it offers, but the frugal homesteader thinks very carefully before forking over cash, opting instead to trade and barter wherever possible.

So the first thing to understand is that being a modern homesteader means NOT being a modern consumer.

The ideal situation is that you are now thinking of becoming a homesteader but have not transitioned yet. You hope to make the leap down the road… say, in a year or two, unless, if you are concerned about such things, TEOTWAWKI (The End Of The World As we Know It) forces everyone's hand sooner! Or perhaps you are already homesteading or micro-farming but are in search of ideas to generate more money. If either of these is your situation, below are the priorities and actions as I see them to help you to prepare for successful modern homesteading.

ELIMINATE ALL DEBT

If you are like almost every American, you are in debt to some degree. This makes almost all of us, if not slaves, at least captives of the industrial machine, and requires that we stay put, labor to earn a paycheck and continually service the debt. Almost all of us are in this condition… the entire country is. We use credit for mortgages, furniture, automobiles, appliances, school, health care, home improvement and, to perpetuate the problem, for consolidating other debts we owe!

Our society seems to collectively embrace using debt to enjoy today what we failed to save for yesterday. Whereas our parents and grandparents may have left college unencumbered with degrees in hand and walked straight into a waiting job, today we leave laden with heavy debt and, with no jobs waiting, occasionally to occupy city parks to represent 99 percent of the population. Debt becomes part of our life and few of us are ever able to jump off the treadmill that propels us to always chase more income just to keep up.

Of course, if you have amassed a lot of debt, it is easier said than done to get out of debt. Nevertheless, the task awaits and the sooner the debt is discharged, the sooner you will be free.

Therefore, the first step to financial freedom is eliminating debt, and that step begins with a change in mindset.

Rather than dreaming of what you want in the moment and seeking immediate gratification, try to focus on the ultimate goal of homesteading, a goal that is easier to achieve without debt than with. Make your homesteading dream so real that you can almost taste it and it will become easier to forgo the taste of that morning latte, because doing so means you are one dollar closer to your dream.

How?

- Share the goal with your family and friends.
- Visit with and talk to other homesteaders, farmers, and/or preppers whom you admire.
- Find scenic pictures of the life you want and plaster them around your home or cubicle to keep the dream alive.
- Listen to audiobooks or podcasts on homesteading while you are stuck in traffic. I cannot recall how many times we listened to the audio version of Barbara Kingsolver's wonderful book, *Animal, Vegetable, Miracle* as we were planning our transition. Other favorites of ours at the time were Michael Pollan's books, notably *The Omnivore's Dilemma*, and numerous podcasts about going to the country.
- Take time to complete the Homestead Entrepreneurial Life Plan (HELP) included in chapter six.

I described much of our own transition to homesteading in my first book, *The Accidental Farmers*, so I will not go over the story again here. The point is for YOU to keep your homesteading fire burning.

WHAT DO YOU REALLY NEED?

So many people have become conditioned to believe they are entitled to conveniences and luxuries, or the government handouts that are given freely, whereas the homesteading mentality is about happily living on what one produces and does on one's own without borrowing. Bartering? Yes. Borrowing? No.

I urge you to adopt the homestead mentality NOW, prior to making the transition. For every dollar that goes out, ask yourself, "Do I really need to spend this now or could this be saved?" The more money and less debt you have as a homesteader, the less income you need to earn to enjoy your lifestyle.

Once you have adopted the homesteader mindset, you will likely find that those things that occupy so much of your mind-share (and deplete the contents of your wallet) today no longer hold interest for you. This makes the transition to homesteading easier once you reach this level.

Urban (consumption) life seems to "require" many non-essential expenses and distractions, such as:

- Cable/satellite TV,
- Lattes and espressos,
- Newspaper and magazine subscriptions,
- Dining out,
- Gym memberships,
- Expensive furniture,
- Fancy cars,
- Clothes,
- Tobacco and alcohol,
- Movies/sports/concerts,
- HOA fees,

- Lodging/vacations,
- Pet care,
- Shiny appliances,
- Repairs to shiny appliances,
- Pest control,
- Lawn services,
- Water bills,
- and so on.

Our ancestors required virtually none of these a few generations ago. As a result, they were not required to earn as much, so, for the most part, had no debt.

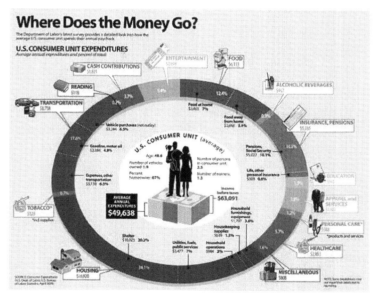

If your experience mirrors that of most modern homesteaders, you will ultimately end up incurring very few of these expenses, and certainly not miss anything. Therefore, take whatever steps you can to start practicing this now. Instead of missing TV, modern homesteaders become distracted by reading, nature, DIY projects and the pleasures of growing their own food. You can too!

While the Internet may be seen as a very real necessity for homesteaders, particularly given their isolation and need to connect with friends, family, and customers, that one expense can be used to consolidate and minimize other expenses. Some homesteaders use a single Internet bill to access news, information and free video programs via Hulu, YouTube, iTunes and elsewhere, thereby eliminating bills elsewhere. All the above expenses seem "necessary" to us as urbanites, but viewed through a homesteader's lens, they are quite unnecessary indeed. What role do they play in sustaining you and helping you achieve your self-sufficient independence? If you cannot cut the cord and do without them where you are now, the homesteading life may not be for you.

> NOTE: This book DOES NOT attempt to provide debt management or financial guidance. Rather, it underscores the importance of doing everything you can to eliminate existing debt and avoid future debt. Some people profiled in this book have reported success by reading and following Dave Ramsey's books and methods, including his book *The Total Money Makeover*. If you need help with debt management, this is a book that seems to have helped others, as the following profile suggests.

Like many people, Brian and Stephanie Larsen heard a more self-sufficient lifestyle calling them, but high levels of debt threatened their dream. Here is the inspiring story of how they confronted that burden head on and overcame the obstacle.

PROFILE # 1

"We feel elated to have conquered our debt and to have a paid-for property."

– Stephanie Larsen

Who: Brian and Stephanie Larsen, www.thewannabehomesteader.com

Where: North Central Florida

Homestead/Farm Highlights: We live in a mobile home on a quarter-acre of land that is 100 percent paid for. We are remodeling the mobile home and modernizing it, cash-flowing the process rather than doing it on credit cards. We have chickens and meat rabbits and hope to get into beekeeping, fruit trees, and gardening.

What inspired (or scared) you into pursuing a more self-sufficient lifestyle? We were both inspired and scared by different situations into leading a more self-sufficient lifestyle. I wanted to live a healthier life and feed my family local, organic food. After learning how expensive that can be, we got into gardening and chicken keeping. Producing organic food is inspiring because it's better for the environment and for our family's health. At the same time, we feel the need to be prepared for man-made and natural disasters, inflation, and social upheaval.

When you made your move to homesteading, were family and friends supportive? Yes. My dad and uncle were thinking the same way and taking steps to live a more self-sufficient lifestyle. We shared our concerns and plans.

What are your income streams now? Our blog makes a small income and most of our steady income comes from Brian's employment as a helicopter mechanic.

How did you go about getting out of debt to finance your dream of homesteading? Getting out of debt took us five years. We were $60k in debt with only one income that averaged $45k. We followed Dave Ramsey's debt snowball plan, read his books, and listened to his radio show for encouragement. Brian is the "nerd" (the saver) and I was the "free spirit" (the spender) so we had to come together to accomplish this. I had to learn delayed gratification, patience, and faith. We had nothing and still did without a lot of things. Facing debt head-on is not for the weak. Thankfully, Brian had the dedication and self-control that I did not.

Now that you are completely out of debt and own your own home, what does that mean to you? How do you feel now compared to at the peak of your debt? We feel elated to have conquered our debt and to have a paid-for property. However, this is only a starter property and not our dream property. We have very little in terms of assets. Before, we were $60k in the hole and now we feel we are at Point Zero. We do not have debt putting us in the negative but we also have very little in "the positive." We feel more responsible and secure than we did at the peak of our debt but we still have a lot of work to do.

Starting a website (blog or otherwise) can be intimidating to people who are not used to that sort of thing. How did you learn to create a blog and why do you do it? I began blogging right after the "first wave" of ordinary folks (people just like me) started their blogs, had been blogging to a couple of years, and were now self-professed "experts" at it. They offered their experiences and hacks for the rest of us. Sites like Problogger.com were already there to help newbies like myself through the ins and outs of blogging. Besides that, blogging is mainly just trial and error. I like to write and I want to share my personal experiences to offer encouragement for people who are in debt (like we were) but want a more self-sufficient lifestyle.

If starting over again on the path to self-sufficiency, what would you do differently? If we could start over, we would have put more time and energy into learning how to grow fruits and vegetables earlier on. Florida is one of the hardest locations there is to grow food organically. The learning curve has been steep for us. You cannot learn to grow food in one season.

What do you miss about city/urban life...you know, the "real" world? I miss the cultural diversity, especially regarding cuisines. Country life is great but we just do not have the variety of restaurants, tastes, and flavors that urban areas have. We love sushi and Asian food and it is just not here in the woods!

Finally, what advice do you have for someone considering leaving a "real job" to become more self-sufficient? Make sure your finances are in order and you have no debt. A paid-for piece of property (and shelter) should be a requirement if you are planning to give up a secure income to venture "off grid."

LEARN TO GARDEN

Learn to garden now, TODAY, before you make the transition to homesteading! Regardless of the income-producing paths you choose, one thing is common to all homesteaders; they all garden and grow at least some of their own food. Another common thing is this; learning to grow food takes A LOT longer than most new gardeners realize, particularly on a new homestead with virgin garden soil. So any practice you can get today with pest management, planting and transplanting, soil building, building garden beds, composting, seed starting and seed saving and so on will pay substantial dividends for you when you are out on your own.

A popular product these days is survival seed banks. These non-GMO heirloom seed banks appeal as an insurance policy of sorts to those who fear "something bad" may happen. Personally, I think they are a good idea and we keep lots of seeds stored ourselves, but I fear too many people who purchase these products neglect to hone their growing skills. These people are in for a rude awakening when they finally put the seeds into the ground and find that, oops… the seed does not germinate. They scratch their heads, not appreciating that their weather, soil tilth and nutrients, lack of trap plants and presence of pests are unique. They are shocked to find things do not usually work the way the instructions say they should.

No matter where you are currently living, you should be able to practice some gardening. Perhaps there are other gardeners in your area or even a gardening club where you can learn to plan a garden, plant and germinate seeds indoors, transplant into small raised beds or container gardens, learn to improve soil and to identify and manage pests, practice companion planting and square-foot gardening if you are keen on a small parcel, or planting in raised beds if room allows, and so on. Or, perhaps you can volunteer on a local farm.

Also, do not focus solely on vegetables. Practice with small fruits such as strawberries, raspberries, blueberries, and even dwarf-fruit trees grown in containers (that you can take with you when you finally move). By the time you get to your ideal homestead, you will be comforted by the hands-on gardening skills you have practiced and the knowledge gained through reading.

GET YOURSELF IN SHAPE

By this I do not mean do more crunches and bicep curls. Sure, those are great if you are trying to look good on club night, but the cows on the homestead will not give you a second glance. For those unaccustomed to the work, homesteading takes a toll on the body. Your tasks will likely include bending and kneeling to weed and plant, hoisting 50-pound or heavier bags of feed while balancing them over a feeder, carrying crates of chickens, shoveling compost or wet snow, chopping firewood, bending over cheese vats, lifting heavy, wet trays of veggies out of the sink to prepare for canning, unloading trucks and tables at the farmers market and so on.

To make matters worse, if you are injured while on the job, you will have no one to call to inform you cannot make it in that day. There are no "sick days" out here, sorry. So best get your body ready for what lies ahead.

How? Well, imagine living 50,000 years ago. What activities would you be performing and what would your body look like as a result? It is unlikely that you would have been carrying excess pounds, and what pounds you did carry would likely be firm, strong, and lean rather than soft, weak, and flappy. Thriving in that environment would have demanded that you be quite nimble, athletic, and very active. I can easily imagine my "primal self" alternating between slow stalking and flat-out sprints as I covered five miles a day or more, balancing myself on rugged terrain and flexing my back as I tugged stubborn roots from the ground or dragged big game to my "tiny cabin."

The sedentary lifestyle most of us live today is diametrically opposed to the active primal lifestyle I just described. Even those who do embrace fitness today often focus on what looks good rather than what works well. We have all seen examples of people with biceps twice as big as their calves as a result of doing endless bicep curls. That is fine, I suppose, but biceps do not come in as handy on the farm as strong legs, a good back, and flexibility. Equally important is maintaining weight at the right target level for your age and height.

So, given that we are not stalking (or fleeing) wild beasts every day, what exercise movements are best to help us achieve the physical capabilities of our primal selves? Below are seven movements that I believe are far better to prepare you for life on the homestead than any number of crunches or bicep curls. If you are unfamiliar with them, please look them up (after you consult with your doctor about your level of fitness, of course).

1. **Squatting** – Plant both feet on the ground, bend your legs so you lower your body as you keep your chest up and lower back straight. Just as you use squatting to sit in a chair, you will use it often on the homestead as you weed, lift, and in some cases, leap.

2. **Lunging** – Our "primal selves" would have used lunging to heave a spear or carry water while stepping over a downed tree, and you will use it plenty on the homestead too. Just step forward with one leg and bend it while keeping the other leg stationary.

3. **Pushing** – Think push ups. If that is too hard, you can push against a wall at first and increase the angle over time so that you are pushing more weight. I have had to push many a new cow into the milking parlor for their first milking. The problem with being so friendly to your cows is that, sometimes, they just will not move no matter what you do. Pushing helps.

4. **Pulling** – And, we have had to pull many calves. If you have

never done this, you will be surprised how much pulling effort it takes. Once, it took three adults using all our collective might to pull out a calf! Other times we are pulling large tree branches off fences. Get your gang together and practice a weekly tug of war; it will prepare you for what is to come. Or if it is raining, just grab a dumbbell and do a single dumbbell row.

5. **Twisting** – Practice twisting by sitting on the floor, raising your feet slightly off the floor and twisting your torso right to left. To increase your strength and agility, perform this while holding a weight against your chest. Or better yet, pick up a 25-pound truckle of cheddar cheese and twist between the shelves and the table as you brush it.

6. **Bending** – Oh boy, will you do some bending out here. Digging and pulling potatoes, planting, feeding, weeding, seeding... you name it. Get your back in shape NOW, for any soreness or injuries you experience while homesteading means that work will not get done.

7. **Accelerating** – Walking and jogging are common activities, but you will not find yourself doing a lot of jogging on the farm. Rather, you will walk or you will sprint when your cows or sheep break out again and you need to get ahead of them before they hit the pavement and the sheriff visits you. Again. Of course, our "primal selves" would have sprinted a great deal and, if you get used to doing it, you will get the added benefit of being fit and trim. Ever see any flabby sprinters?

FEED YOUR BRAIN AND FIND LIKE-MINDED SOULS

For millennia, knowledge passed from elders to juniors in social circles so that succeeding generations understood important food production, preservation, and survival skills. Unfortunately, most of us missed out on that transfer of knowledge as our parents and grandparents were lured instead into the convenience generation that food marketers carefully (and profitably) cultivated.

So how do we regain those lost skills?

Start by reading as much as you can. The problem is sifting through all the sources of information available in books such as this one, blogs such as selfsufficientblog.com and countless others, articles and magazines. A list of many excellent resources appears at the end of this book. Your study assignments go even beyond reading to watching movies and videos, and listening to podcasts. The choices are many and it can be hard to find exactly what you want, so to start, I suggest finding topics that intrigue you and then learning as much as you can about them.

Once you find something that appeals to you, get involved with a forum or group and start talking with your virtual buddies. For example, if you are interested in cheese-making, there is a great forum of hundreds (if not thousands) of homestead and professional cheesemakers at cheeseforum.org. Likewise, there are many other sites particular to brewing, gardening, prepping and more, so find them and get involved. However, since you are interested in earning income rather than only pursuing a hobby, seek out those who have ideas about and experience of making money. Remember, that is the point of this book; your goal is to uncover ways to make money so you can live your self-sufficient life. Otherwise, the hobby you are passionate about could end up being a cash drain. As a farmer once said to me, "There is a lot of money in farming. I know, because I put it in there." Learn from that farmer's experience by seeking others who produce profitable income streams.

If you are hooked on Facebook, stop using it to upload your latest selfie. Instead, if you must use it, do so to find and follow pages that can give you practical knowledge and encouragement, such as pages on DIY, canning and food preservation, preparedness, homesteading, tiny house living and so on. Do not just look at the pictures. Actually put into practice those things you read about.

Physical alternatives to the virtual world include local food groups, organic farming associations, farming conferences, prepper events, classes/workshops and more. Find people who share your ideals and who are searching for the same answers. Networking will get you there much faster and will open your eyes to new possibilities. Talk to people who have taken a similar journey and ask them to share their story. Find people who have learned the skills you seek and reach out to them. Ask them for resources or see if they would be willing to let you watch a homestead activity the next time they do one, such as making soap or collecting honey, for instance! Do not be bashful about attending all the farm tours and events you can find.

The author leading a farm tour at Nature's Harmony Farm

FIND YOUR PASSION

Why exactly do you want to homestead or farm? What excites you and what do you want to do? Do you long to grow the best tomatoes and sell directly to leading chefs? Do you covertly want to hide from overhead drones and simply feed your family? Do you want to be the next Joel Salatin and have a farm of chicken tractors, eggmobiles and salad bar beef?

Of course, there is no right answer but there are wrong ones, those being the ones you are not passionate about. Without passion, your homesteading adventure will become a laborious job for you. Sure, the idea of being surrounded by chicken tractors may seem great to you now but have you spent much time pulling them up irregular terrain every day, in the rain, hauling feed and removing dead chickens as needed? Oh, yes… there are mortalities on the farm that you will have to deal with, something I shared in great detail in *The Accidental Farmers.*

If you are not up for animal husbandry, then veggies or crafts may be more your cup of tea. Many homesteaders, including Patrice Lewis who is profiled in chapter four, have achieved success centering their homestead on a home-based craft business. Anna Hess and Mark Hamilton, profiled in chapter three, launched a successful business selling automatic chicken waterers, while Herrick Kimball, profiled in chapter four, combined his passion for homesteading, engineering, and writing to teach people to create chicken pluckers and other Whizbang products. Spend some time now daydreaming about what YOU want. Actually picture yourself doing these tasks and be honest about whether you will be happy doing this every day for years to come. Either way, find out what you truly love and then set out to do it.

One way to get a taste of farm life is to seek a farm apprenticeship or internship if you can find one, or to volunteer on local farms if they will have you. How can you find farm apprenticeships? Try WWOOF (World Wide Opportunities on Organic Farms) and become a WWOOFer! According to their website, "WWOOF connects people who want to live and learn on organic farms with people who are looking for volunteer help." I can attest to the WWOOF experience as we have used several WWOOFers on our farm and we each had a great experience.

If the WWOOF experience is too much for you, consider a one-day crop mob such as Crop Mob Georgia or a similar group near you. Or, just keep your eyes open for farm volunteer days in your area that you can be part of.

A quick comment on asking to help on a farm… be understanding when you approach farmers who have not advertised a volunteer or apprenticeship opening. You may wonder why your act of generous volunteer labor is not immediately accepted, but realize that it is actually a disruption in the daily routine and more work for the farmers to teach you chores or answer questions when you "help" for a few days or less. Having said that, many farmers are invigorated by being able to inspire or tutor someone with a genuine interest and respectful approach.

FOCUS ON LASTING INVESTMENTS

There are many things you may want to retain or acquire before becoming a homesteader that will help you once you are on the land. There may also be items you want to trade in for something more practical. For example, how about trading your shiny compact car for a good, solid, used diesel truck that you can ultimately use without worry of scratching? In addition to saving money when buying and insuring this truck, you will find it useful for hauling animals, seed, feed, fertilizer, tools… you name it. Being an older model, it will be less complicated to repair and keep running than your current vehicle.

If there are ANY new items you are considering buying between the time you read this sentence and the time you move to the land, ask yourself this question: is this item essential to my homesteading dream? If not, perhaps you do not need it. If you can afford it, then the choice is yours, but make sure it will be a lasting investment that is well worth the expense. After all, modern homesteading is not about deprivation; it is about fulfillment. If you are not sure how to afford living off the land, then consider postponing any discretionary expenses until you figure it out.

GET SOME LAND

I realize that sounds obvious… I mean, after all, it is hard to really homestead without at least a little land. You do not need that much, but you will probably conclude that you do want some. If you are one of the lucky ones who have inherited land, fantastic. Congratulations! But most of us have to find a way to buy our own land. For a couple of reasons, I believe the time to do that is now.

For one, I believe that rural/farm land prices will only escalate in coming years as we need to produce more and more food to feed a rapidly expanding global population. For another, if you must finance the land, interest rates remain at absurdly (and artificially) low levels as I am writing this book. As you will read repeatedly throughout this book, I encourage you to live as debt-free as possible. However, it would be false to suggest that successful businesses cannot be built with the intelligent use of debt; in fact, most often, this is the case. If your goal is to build a business and you have a plan to generate sufficient income to service the debt, I think it is unlikely you will see interest rates lower than they currently are again in your lifetime.

The Internet makes it far easier than it used to be to search for land. Many sites, including landwatch.com, landflip.com, landandfarm. com, landsofamerica.com and many others allow you to search nationwide for your dream property. Do not rely solely on these sites, however, as many properties are not listed there and can instead be better discovered through an excellent real estate agent if you know what area you are interested in. Also, remember to check foreclosed properties on foreclosure.com where you may find a great deal!

Think carefully about how much land you want and need, and how the composition of the land impacts your income potential and workload. For example, many new farmers/homesteaders have starry-eyed visions of a large property, but may fail to fully realize the amount of human energy it will take to maintain and work the acreage. Alternatively, if they purchase land with minimal pasture and lots of woodlot, the workload will be greatly reduced, as will the land's income potential.

BUT YOU DO NOT *HAVE* TO GET LAND!

Okay, so you hear the voice of self-sufficiency calling you, but for whatever reason, are not able or willing to secure a piece of land in the wilderness. What do you do? You do what you can to embrace self-sufficient living!

While this book is about how to generate income as a homesteader, there are many ways you can embrace the homesteading spirit, regardless of whether you have land.

For example, even if you are confined within a tiny apartment, you can still:

- Buy ingredients at a farmers market, learn recipe ratios and how to cook from scratch,
- Learn to bake bread from scratch,
- Learn how to preserve food (dehydrating, water-bath canning, pressure canning, etc.) AND practice food preservation,
- Take trips in season to hunt, fish, track, trap, and bring back meat to preserve,
- Learn to make your own soap, shampoo, cleaning supplies, and even medicines from medicinal herbs you purchase online or at markets,
- Practice bartering,
- Practice community-building by seeking other city/apartment dwellers who wish to embrace the homesteading spirit,
- Learn to sew and make some of your own clothes, or at least to mend them,

- Practice seed starting and container gardening. In fact, if you want a REAL taste of gardening, put some heavy clay in those containers on your balcony rather than fluffy potting mix so you can practice with real-world conditions,
- Teach yourself to make cheese, butter, yogurt, charcuterie, etc. or take local classes to learn those skills,
- Take classes on animal butchering at local farms/butcher shops,
- Participate in Consumer Supported Agriculture (CSA) with a local farm and/or volunteer at local farms to learn growing and animal husbandry skills,
- Above all, practice living more frugally. Stop consuming and start producing!

Of course, the more space you have, the more you can do. In addition to the above, if you live in a typical suburban lot, you may be able to raise a few chickens or rabbits, hang your clothes out to dry, practice square-foot or raised-bed gardening, practice permaculture and plant edible landscapes and more. If you have a Homeowner's Association (HOA), you will have to abide by its rules, but there is still much you can do and embrace.

Homesteading does not have to be all or nothing. Certainly, many (if not most) of the income-generation ideas presented in this book do not require you to own or rent land. In fact, read the profile later in this chapter of BubbaTanicals and learn how Brian and Laura Tant embraced homesteading and created a homestead-based business, even as they retained their jobs and spent many hours snarled in Atlanta traffic!

PROFILE # 2

"I came to discover that living in a world of glass and concrete was thin and fake compared to the simple joys of picking blueberries barefooted in the dew-soaked grass."

– Brian Tant

Who: Brian and Laura Tant, founders of BubbaTanicals.com, a farm crafts company that sells handmade natural soaps, jams & jellies, eggs, honey, produce, and goat's milk products.

Where: Brooks, Georgia

What was your "real job" prior to breaking away to become more self-sufficient? I have been in corporate IT since the ripe age of 17. At 39, I still work full time as a security consultant. It is a job I enjoy, and it pays too well to walk away from just yet. Laura teaches in a local elementary school and still derives tremendous fulfillment from working with young children. So we have yet to fully "break away." Our homestead is a long-term step in a journey. We are going to be here awhile but we also know that the land around us will continue to develop. We are positioning ourselves to take advantage of the right opportunity when the time comes.

What inspired you to start down the road to becoming more self-sufficient? Laura grew up in rural Georgia and has always had a green thumb. She grew up a country girl and brings out the best in me. We went to high school together. When we started dating seriously, I came to discover that living in a world of glass and concrete was thin and fake compared to the simple joys of picking blueberries barefooted in the dew-soaked grass. I moved in with her and we lived on a farm with her parents before buying our own piece of land. I came to deeply appreciate the simple rhythm of the seasons, and it felt natural to live more by the cues of the nature than by a company calendar. I realized this was the life I wanted to build.

Laura has always been a talented gardener and often, her gardens grow beyond their design. I came out of the house one afternoon to find her tearing through a large patch of mint with a weed eater. I thought, *this is the same mint people pay money for!* That was the first time I considered agriculture as a business venture. I started a company called Willow Point Herbals, named after her parents' estate. It was marginally profitable but I knew nothing about business. We soon ran into issues with sporadic supply not keeping up with yearlong demand. We sold at a few local shops, but quality control was difficult. We had a barn full of herbs that baked in the Georgia summer, quickly degrading our overhead. All the while we were dabbling in ways to diversify our offerings.

Homestead/Farm Highlights: We have a ten-acre homestead in Brooks, GA. It is divided into three small pastures that we rotate our grazers through. We have planted peaches, muscadines, blueberries, blackberries, apples, dewberries, elderberries, figs, and a huge menagerie of perennial herbs. We also cultivate the typical annual veggies such as peppers, tomatoes, squashes, melons, beans, etc. The critter population consists of two horses, four goats, about thirty chickens, three dogs, three cats, worm beds, and several bee hives. We use the fruits for jams and wine. The bees give us honey, pollen, propolis, wax, and more bees to sell. The goats provide weed control, milk, and baby goats—which we sell. The dogs control most predators, and the cats handle rodents. The worms provide castings and supplement the chickens. The chickens provide meat and eggs and my daughters use the horses in competitions, fox hunting and trail riding. Everything has a purpose and we try to use these elements for as many different things as possible to overlap functions and benefits.

What are your income streams: how do you generate income, including off-farm? We sell our products online, directly, and at a local farmers market. We can only sell the soaps online due to government regulations, but locally we sell honey, eggs, goats-milk products, jams, and jellies. We also have been known to occasionally do a workshop or two on processing chickens and beekeeping.

Why did you choose part-time urban homesteading versus a full-time rural property? We live in an affluent area with good schools, which makes for a higher than average cost of living. We have three kids, one in college, and another starting next year. We need a steady income that can support our existing lifestyle and put our kids through school. Plus I am still learning about what makes a successful business. I have tried to position BubbaTanicals in such a way that it is small enough to be manageable part-time, but can be grown to a modest full-time concern in a relatively short time if needed or desired.

Why did you choose a soap-making business, and how did you learn to make soap? My middle daughter developed some minor eczema several years ago for which the dermatologist suggested switching to natural skin care products. That is when soap entered the picture. We started with natural melt and pour bases and soon found they helped my daughter as well as any ointment, and that there was a surprisingly consistent demand for them.

Soap allowed us to use the natural herbals in a way that increased their shelf life without degrading quality. We priced out other natural soap at boutique places and saw that it sold for ridiculous prices, but was often full of not-so-natural ingredients such as laurate, sulfate, and synthetic fragrances. I knew we could do it better and cheaper. We could put premium soap into the hands of people who still used Irish Spring. We soon moved into cold process soap making using simple recipes. Encouraged by our success, we transitioned entirely out of whole herbs and into soap making. From there I eventually learned the subtle techniques of swirling, how the various oils trace, steeping the herbs, using essential oils, etc. I came up with a new brand that spoke to our natural ingredients and country lifestyle: BubbaTanicals, Good Soap. No Crap.

Starting a business for the first time can be scary. How did you market your soap products and get customers? When we transitioned into soap making, we already had a small customer base. I work full time so I did not really need the income at the time. This allowed me to step back and really examine how I chose whom to do business with. I found that I hate dealing with faceless businesses. I like to deal with people, and I dealt with them because I knew them and there was a level of trust. I bought from the person, not the business. That was the model I chose. I decided I would run the business with no regard for any single transaction, that all decisions would be made from the perspective that the customer is a family friend and should be treated as such. We have probably given away thousands of dollars' worth of products to cultivate those relationships, and that is just fine. Customers share their stories, and I always put a handwritten thank you note in every order. I try to know the person. A woman once told me in tears that her mother was in chemotherapy and that our goats milk soap was the only thing that did not irritate her skin. I sent her a year's worth of product the next day. I took a loss, absolutely. But it was a chance to really help someone. The real value is in the relationship, not the sale. The bottom line is that it is valuable to do right by people, especially when your competition will not. That woman has since referred dozens of customers to us. Genuine word of mouth marketing is not something you can buy.

We started a podcast that quickly gained a surprising degree of popularity. While I hesitate to call this marketing, it was, because we use it to put ourselves out there. The podcast is an outreach to build rapport with people and show them that the brand is backed by real people. We talk about what we do, how we do it, and try to just be genuine. If someone wants to seek out a similar lifestyle, we're here to share our story. We have made many friends, and are always humbled when a listener says the show has helped them in some way.

If starting over again on the path to self-sufficiency, what would you do differently? I would have a short-term and long-term design. We wasted time and money in the school of hard knocks. I would also have taken the physical demands of developing productive land more seriously.

What do you miss about city/urban life...you know, the "real" world? Being close to the earth and knowing your neighbors is far more "real" than anything in an urban setting. The urban world seems to have to continuously invent distractions to keep people from going back to the land. But the urban homestead phenomenon has seen tremendous growth in recent years. Chickens, bees, rabbits, and small gardens are infiltrating the concrete jungles of our cities. I believe people were meant to know the Earth, and will always be drawn to have that connection in their lives.

What advice do you have for someone considering leaving a "real job" to become more self-sufficient? Treat it like a business. Everything costs more than you think and you do not realize how much income you spend on modern indulgences. Get out of debt, look at what lifestyle changes you are willing to make, and do a dry run to get a taste of them. You will find many modern conveniences you have grown accustomed to require hard work to maintain. Self-sufficiency is a long-term learning process. Cultivate alternate income streams to buffer setbacks along the way, because you may find that going all in is not what you really want. Maybe it is. You can only know by trying it out. Also, leaving a real job should not be a one-day event. Life changes are better weathered when are they deliberate transitions.

23 QUESTIONS TO ANSWER BEFORE BUYING RURAL PROPERTY

When you begin searching for rural property, you will quickly find all sorts of places that look promising to you. Mountain views, green pastures, ponds with cattails, all idyllic landscapes that connect with that inner voice you have been hearing. Before you plunk down that deposit on the first property that screams your name, consider this: you are planning to make a move there for life. A new life, a better life and, perhaps, not only the rest of your life but a homestead that future generations will cherish. So it is definitely appropriate to take some time and weigh the decision against criteria that are important to you and your family. With this in mind, I encourage you to ask yourself the following questions when looking for a new homestead:

1. **How much land do you need?** You can homestead on less than an acre if that is your goal. Many people do. However, do you want livestock? Orchards? If so, what do you want?

Chickens and rabbits require very little land, sheep and goats require a little more and cows require, at a minimum, one or two acres of dedicated pasture each... and that is IF you are in good pasture/rainfall areas typical of the eastern United States. In much of the western United States more land is required, often much more. If you are thinking about having horses, get far more land than you think—10 acres per horse (in the east) in addition to your house, driveway, garden, etc.

2. **Can you COMFORTABLY afford the land**? Only you know how much you can afford for the home and land. Can you purchase the land and be debt-free? If not, can you comfortably afford the down payment with plenty of financial reserves left over to deal with the unexpected? How much will any improvements to the land or buildings cost?

3. **How is the water**? Does the land have excellent water? (I encourage you to make this a very high priority.) Does the water come from a natural spring or has a well been drilled? If it is a spring, is it located above the elevation of the house and garden so you can use gravity for water distribution? If the water is from a well, how many gallons per minute does it produce AND what is the static water depth? For example, in our case, we have a well 300 feet deep that produces over 45 gallons per minute, but the static water depth is less than 40 feet. Have you tested the water quality? If it is raw land have you received an estimate for the cost of drilling a well? Have you ascertained the well depths and flow rates for your closest neighbors so you can have confidence that your well will perform as needed? If you plan on raising livestock, how will you get water to them?

4. **Is there good potential for alternative energy**? Many homesteaders share the dream of completely off-grid, but that is not possible if the land is not conducive to energy

production. If you are considering solar energy, does the land have excellent sun exposure or is it surrounded by dense woods? If you are considering wind or hydro power, is the land suitable for that? Is there a woodlot so you can cut your own firewood?

5. **Do you have a good understanding of the local weather**? How much rain per year does the area receive? More importantly, how frequently does the rain come? For example, we average over 50 inches of rain per year on our homestead, yet we often go through the hottest parts of summer and receive only one to two inches during a three-month period, creating a lot of stress on our livestock and gardens. What are the winters like where you are looking? Summers? How frequently is there drought? Flooding? Tornadoes and hurricanes? Wildfires?

6. **What is the growing season and how long is it**? Have you spoken with other local gardeners and/or agriculture extension offices? Do you know what crops can be grown, when they must be planted and harvested? What kind of fruits can you grow? What kind of pests are you likely to encounter? Do you have skills in all these areas or are you starting from scratch?

7. **What is the community like**? Are there like-minded people? Are there groups or organizations you would like to join? Can you join them BEFORE you move to see first-hand what the people are like? Are there gardening clubs, homeschooling support groups and so on? Just as there are micro-climates in weather, there are also micro-cultures. Did you remember to subscribe to the local newspaper BEFORE making an offer and relocating? If so, how is the help wanted section? Skimpy or full? What does that tell you about the local economy? What about police reports? What crime is in the community

and how close is it to the property you are considering? Are there many foreclosure listings or only a few?

8. **How likely is it the community will drastically change**? Is the town you are considering located between major points of interest that may cause it to grow over time? For example, I grew up in a beautiful mountain town in northern Georgia that was quaint and sparsely populated, with families who had lived in the county for generations. Today, the town is still there but "prosperity" has arrived in the form of fast-food restaurants, souvenir shops, chain coffee shops, and LOTS of traffic. Why? Because a major road that connects Georgia to the Smoky Mountains goes right through the valley where the town is located.

9. **What are the immediate neighbors like**? If you are seriously considering a specific property, have you introduced yourselves to the neighbors before making an offer? Do you share anything in common with them? Children, hobbies, political beliefs, religious views, societal views, etc? Would you invite them over for dinner? Would you want to go to dinner at their house?

10. **How remote is it/how close to town**? One of the best things about homesteading can be seclusion, but, for some, it can also be the worst. How close do you want to be to a town? What do you want out of the town? Simply a store or two? Or are you interested in being close to decent restaurants, yoga studios, pubs, golf courses and the like? There are no right answers, but be honest about what you want and find that community.

11. **What are the characteristics of the specific land you are considering**? Is it flat, gently sloping, or steep mountainside? Is it wide open with no trees or are there wind breaks? How is the soil drainage? If it has pasture, what perennial forages are

growing? Are there also legumes (clovers, vetch, etc.) that can help fix nitrogen to the soil? How is the earthworm activity? Is it only one species of grass, such as Bermuda, or is the pasture a mix of forages? Does the forage match the animals you hope to put on it? For example, if the pasture consists of "old" fescue that is prone to endophytes, it may not be wise to plan on having horses. What is the potential for flooding? Is the garden area positioned for maximum sun exposure? Is the land fenced? Is there a perimeter fence around the entire property? Are the pastures cross-fenced for rotational grazing? If so, are the fences high-tensile, woven-wire field fence, wooden fence or what? What is their condition? How much time will it take you to maintain and mow them?

12. **How was the land previously used**? Regardless of whether the land is beautiful or unkempt, do you know how it was previous used? Were chemicals used and, if so, when were they last applied? What types of fertilizers, if any, were applied? Was the land frequently disked or tilled? Have you sampled a section of land for earthworm activity? Have you confirmed that you will own ALL water and mineral rights?

13. **Have you tested the soil**? You are what you eat, so you will want to know what is in the soil. Have you had it tested? Did you sample several areas of the land and pasture, or only one? What were the recommendations for soil improvement for each area? How long will it take to get the soil where it needs to be based on your planned use for it? For example, if it is acidic, how much lime is required and what is the cost for purchasing and spreading the lime? Is the soil sorely lacking in nutrients that your animals need, such as selenium or manganese? What were the specific recommendations for the garden area? Have you sought the free advice of the local county extension agent?

14. **Who maintains the roads**? Is your new property accessible by nice, maintained roads, or is it accessible only via Class IV (unimproved) roads that you may need to maintain? Is there a driveway to your house or must you install one? Have you considered the costs for gravel, grading, plowing, etc?

15. **Does the land have potential for your plans**? Sure, you may want to start simply with a garden and a dozen chickens, but is it possible you may want to grow your farmstead into something more? If so, will the land accommodate your dreams? Is there room for the cows, sheep, horses, buildings, ponds or whatever visions tease you while sleeping? Is there a sunny spot for the garden or is the land on a mountainside where direct sunlight is measured in minutes rather than hours?

16. **Does the land have usable outbuildings**? If so, what is their condition? Can you afford any repair costs or can you do it yourself? Can the buildings be used for future income-generating ideas that are discussed in this book, such as for classes or events? If so, those may present great value to you but little value to the current owner.

17. **Are there local hospitals and high quality health care**? If you frequently need medical attention, are there hospitals and good doctors within a reasonable driving distance? Is there good emergency care should someone in your family suffer an injury on the farm? Is there adequate dental care?

18. **Is the house (or homesite) properly placed in its environment**? A house snuggled up against the woods sounds great until you find the woods are loaded with copperheads who take a liking to your back porch. If the land has a house on it, is it where you want it? (It is pretty hard to move it later.) Have you really visualized yourself in the home?

Does the house have a swimming pool? Shade trees are nice, but if they are located near the pool, have you considered their location relative to prevailing winds and how that will impact the pool? Is the garden area placed down slope from the house so you can use the house roof to capture rainwater for the garden? If so, where is the septic system relative to the garden area, since it too will be down slope from the house?

19. **Does the land afford the ability to hunt and/or fish**? You may grow much of your own food, but if you enjoy meat, you can also hunt or fish for free. Does your land allow that? Is there an abundance of deer, turkey, wild pigs, freshwater fish or whatever you are interested in? Access to this can dramatically reduce cost of food for you and your animals, as discussed in chapter five.

20. **Are there neighborhood dogs**? If your new land is not securely fenced, are there neighborhood dogs that may enjoy your new chickens or rabbits? Do you know for sure?

21. **Are there other potential hazards of the location you are considering**? I have mentioned snakes, but what about other wildlife such as bears and wolves? Are you in a frequent tornado or hurricane risk area? Is there poisonous vegetation that could harm you (or your animals), such as poison sumac, poison ivy, poison oak, wild cherry trees (can be poisonous to livestock), pasture grasses high in prussic acid (grazed improperly, this can be deadly to cattle), etc? While not necessarily a "hazard," are there nuisances such as fire ants or seasonal gnats and/or mosquitos that could spread disease? What about disease-spreading ticks? I do not mean to alarm you, but embracing the beauty of self-sufficient life means embracing all of nature.

22. **Are there zoning restrictions**? Covenants? HOAs? My recommendation is to not move anywhere that has a HOA

or any covenants, but that is your choice. Regardless, are there local zoning restrictions? Can you later open a bed and breakfast or offer farm dinners/classes if you want? Can you erect barns and simple farm structures without a permit (and fees), or is that required for even the most simple structure? Believe me, you may not begin planning on any of these things, but growing the farmstead becomes additive for many, and may for you as well.

23. **Did you rent or camp in the area prior to making an offer**? If you are unfamiliar with the area, did you rent or camp in the area for an extended time first? Are you certain this is the community for you? After all, you do not want to hate your new home!

Well, okay maybe there are more than 23 questions listed above and I am confident you will add additional questions of your own, but I encourage you to consider these questions carefully. Clearly, purchasing a rural property and leaving "normal" life behind to become more self-sufficient represents a major life decision. It may be one of the most important decisions you ever make and, therefore, deserves careful consideration. Still, having made that move myself years ago, I highly recommend the lifestyle and would never "go back." I do not know anyone who would!

Getting land is an undertaking in itself, though. The region and climate deserve strong consideration, since so much of homesteading depends on what Mother Nature decides to do and what resources are inherent to the land. There is also that tiny problem of how to pay for land if you are strapped for cash. You may be able to find cheaper land of marginal quality in remote areas that is equal to the equity in your suburban home, so perhaps you could swing a trade. If you are not already a homeowner, then your main focus will be to save for land. Again, this book may be able to help by giving you ideas of ways to earn income.

HOW MUCH INCOME DO YOU REALLY NEED?

No matter what your situation, the answer to this question is critical to realizing your dreams of a self-sufficient life. Therefore, it is important that you calculate how much money you really need to make. While your first thought as you contemplate becoming a homesteader may be "how will I make money?" remember this:

Saving Money = Making Money!

By reducing your expenses and producing much of what you will consume when you homestead, you will find that you do not need to make NEARLY as much as you think you do. After all, how much of your current paycheck goes to food that you will no longer purchase, but rather produce on your own? How much goes to nice clothes, dining out, fuel, and simple luxuries that you will want to do without? How much goes to utility bills you will never pay again if you go off-grid?

So there you have it—a few things to get you thinking before you put the shovel in the ground and start digging the homestead garden. As we move on to chapter two, you will need to honestly address the issue of how much income you really need, as the answer to that question will dictate which of the upcoming income ideas are appropriate for you. In the next chapter I will introduce you to ways you can generate income if you own land, but before we begin, let me share with you the inspirational story of how Wilber's Farm came to life.

PROFILE # 3

> "While we are not rich financially, we are very rich in life experiences full of usable skills that our kids can pass down to future generations."
>
> – Wilber Chavez

Who: Wilber and Carmen Chavez, WilbersFarm.com

Where: Belen, New Mexico

If you had a "real job" prior to breaking away to become more self-sufficient, what was it that you left? We worked in the real estate industry.

Homestead/Farm Highlights: We have five acres. Half is free ranged by many small animals.

What inspired (or scared) you into pursuing a more self-sufficient lifestyle? We were concerned with rising food prices and food safety issues such as contamination and GMOs. We were, and still are, concerned that one day the nation's food supply could collapse and people would struggle to feed their families. We wanted to be in a position where we could feed our family healthy food organically grown in sustainable ways.

When you made your move, were family and friends supportive? Not at all. Most friends and family attacked us and claimed we were doing our children an injustice. They feared we would be taking a huge step backward. Some thought our reasons for living a simpler lifestyle were because of financial difficulties and offered to help us financially to prevent us from taking such drastic measures.

How did you fund your homestead dreams... was debt a problem? While we did not have much debt, we also did not have much funds available for our new venture, so we continued to work outside the farm to fund animal living areas and purchase animals for breeding purposes. We started small with what we had and slowly replaced outside income with income earned from our farm venture. Our home is still financed and we pay on one vehicle. We pay cash for everything that cannot be bartered for.

What are your income streams? We try to be as creative as possible and have tried many things. Since we raise many small animals, we cater to others looking for breeding stock to begin or continue their own venture. We have also become a source to those who refuse to buy eggs or meat from supermarkets. While we do not sell processed meat, we sell live animals for others to process themselves. We are always looking for ways to fund our lifestyle and some of the other ways available to us are selling vegetables at farmers markets, and goat milk products to family members. We planted an orchard and soon that will not only be a source of food for us but also provide income from fruit sales.

We also provide handyman services to nearby like-minded neighbors as well as house-cleaning services.

Had you raised small livestock (rabbits, chickens, etc.) before, or was this a new venture for you? This was a new venture for us but we have both been exposed to small and large livestock as children and therefore our passion has always been there. For the first part of my life, the only food we knew was food grown or raised at the farm so a few of the methods have always stayed somewhat fresh in our minds.

How did you acquire the knowledge (and confidence) to begin breeding and selling livestock at Wilber's Farm? Most knowledge came from reading the experiences of others who were ahead of what we wanted to do. As a child I was involved in some of the process of growing and raising food, so we had some general idea. The rest came from trial and error.

Starting a business for the first time can be scary. How did you market your products to get customers? Do you have a marketing background? We had limited marketing experience, but from many years in sales we have learned that most of those experiences carry over to selling and marketing farm related products. Only thing that really differed was finding the clientele that would benefit from our products. We exposed our products to as many like-minded individuals as possible by means of farmers markets, swap meets, and building relationships with feed stores or mills. All the customers buying feed are perfect candidates for animals we sell. They do not mind recommending you to all their feed-buying customers, and the more customers they refer to us, the more we refer back to them as their source of feed for the animals we sell.

If starting over again on the path to self-sufficiency, what would you do differently? More patience. At the beginning we wanted to hit the ground running and after acquiring breeding stock waiting for the breeding process seemed like eternity and the cost of feeding those animals to get them to breeding age and then reproduce seemed overwhelming. The other regret is not starting on the path of self-sufficiency sooner and also quitting our jobs sooner. After we had momentum, the number one reason that held us back was fear, and therefore we hung on to our jobs longer than necessary and hindered our progress.

If relevant, what do you miss about city/urban life...you know, the "real" world? Absolutely nothing. Looking back, we feel bad for city folks being forced to work for unethical corporations, brainwashed to eat tainted produce full of pesticides and food from factory farms. To us, city folks appear imprisoned and manipulated into thinking that is the only way. Kids are more focused on video games and social media rather than being interested in chasing chickens around the farm or hunting for lizards around the land. I really wish everyone could experience all the beauty outside the city. While we are not rich financially, we are very rich in life experiences full of usable skills that our kids can pass down to future generations. We tend to love the city more now from a distance than we did when we lived in one. We look forward to going to the city for needed supplies, visit family, or for entertainment. It is very exciting going to the city now since it is only sparingly, but we would never move back. Of course, now, our workday continues well into after hours, holidays, and weekends but it is very rewarding to witness the birth of a piglet or baby goat even at 11pm. These experiences make it all worth it because we are welcoming a new family member rather than slaving away for someone else.

Finally, what advice do you have for someone considering leaving a "real job" to become more self-sufficient? We believe we have all been blessed with skills and talents that will drive us to succeed in a self-sufficient lifestyle. Things come naturally once all the distractions are removed and you discover abilities and desires you did not know you had. The more people who do this, the easier it will be for everyone who does, because we can support one another and try to live on a barter system like past generations did. If it is your desire to quit your job and move out to the country, then go for it! You can always go back to your old city life, but the regret of not doing something you desired would haunt you for the rest of your life. This is how God designed life to be and it is more rewarding to go with the grain than against it.

Chapter Two
Make Money With Your Land

"It is not because things are difficult that we do not dare; It is because we do not dare that they are difficult."

—Seneca

Chapter one covered areas I believe are important for you to consider and prepare for before transitioning to the homestead. I hope you have carefully considered the last question raised: "How much income do you really need?"

The answer greatly determines which of the following income-producing opportunities are most appropriate to you. Stated simply, if you have zero debt and a small house with no children, very low taxes, and minimal utility costs, then you probably need very little income. This reality will allow you to pick and choose the income options more freely. Conversely, if you have a sizable mortgage, large acreage with a hefty tax bill and are funding college bills, then your income needs are more substantial. This is why so much emphasis is placed on eliminating debt and getting fixed costs to as low a level as possible.

I encourage you to think not of living off the land but rather "thriving" off the land. In time you will learn how to produce your own organic food so your health and nutrition thrive, which is great, but what about income?

For many of us, financial success with homesteading centers on multiple streams of income… the old "do not put all your eggs in one basket" concept, and there is a good reason why this expression is so widely used. Many opportunities exist for generating income on the homestead, but of course there is no single "right" answer given the differences in personal situations, markets, climates, inherent skills and so on. While some homesteaders hope to live frugally and simply on the land, and many do, others have created multi-million dollar enterprises. These include large, sustainable farms and grass-fed meat operations, some large artisan cheese businesses, preparedness websites and consulting businesses, just to name a few. Of course, I have no way of knowing if your goal is to generate $10,000 per year in income or $1,000,000, so this book casts a wide net. What I attempt to do is categorize four main areas of profitable homesteading (three income generation and one expense reduction) and then break those categories down into ways you can generate a little income or a lot, depending on your needs and risk tolerance.

The four main categories of profitable homesteading are:

1. Making money with your land;

2. Making money with your skills;

3. Making money by selling products from your land; and,

4. Saving money by homesteading (which reduces the need to earn money).

This first chapter will describe ways you can use land to generate income, but before we delve into the actual ways to make money, let us begin with mindset.

THINKING LIKE A HOMESTEADER

As you contemplate each of the income generators in this book, try to evaluate them from multiple perspectives.

*   Is the income opportunity one-time, seasonal, or continuous?

The author with his heritage turkeys

For instance, raising heritage turkeys can be fun, but you will likely only get paid at Thanksgiving, whereas consumers buy pork, soap, cheese, and beef year-round. If you are drawn to one-time or seasonal enterprises such as heritage turkeys, be sure to layer other models over it so that income is realized continuously, if that is what you need.

- Can the income opportunity be scaled if you desire? Do you have enough land to scale your grass-fed beef operation if you desire? If you are making crafts, can these be taught to local workers, and do you have the room to expand that business? Have you considered creating an online business that can be scaled easily?

- Can you overlap operational and income-producing areas to spend less so you keep more? For example, if you raise hogs, then you would benefit from either a large garden (scraps) or local cheese operation (whey) or brewery (spent grain) or bakery (stale bred). This would eliminate or dramatically reduce the need to purchase feed, allowing you to raise the hogs essentially for free.

- Does the income opportunity allow you to differentiate yourself or are there lots of people who can offer the same thing? Are the barriers to entry high or low? Some small farmsteaders begin with a pastured poultry operation, because the resources (land and money) required to start up are small. That same benefit applies to everyone, however, so it will be easy for competitors to quickly emerge once you have created a market. Other farming enterprises, such as farmstead cheesemaking and large grass-fed operations require substantial investment, but promise high profit margins. Some online, training and/or consulting businesses require little start-up capital but demand high intellectual capital and life experiences.

- What are you good at now? Can that be transferred to income opportunities on the homestead? When reading all the ideas included in this book, you will likely find you already have experience with something (accounting, writing, graphic and/or web design, woodworking, etc.) that can be parlayed into an income stream.

One income strategy common to many homesteaders that is not covered in this book is that of off-farm income. Frequently, one or more family members will "keep their day job" for income stability, benefit preservation, or simply because it lends itself to rural execution. Indeed, many experienced homesteaders recommend this strategy to "newbies" and you will observe many of the homesteaders profiled in this book employing this strategy. There is nothing wrong with relying on off-farm income and, indeed, it may help to pay off debt while the family transitions to full-time homesteading. However, the meat of this book is devoted to other ways income may be produced from a rural property.

So, are you finally ready to talk money? Good! Me too!

Here are some of the numerous ways you can generate a moderate to great income while living off the land.

Ways to Generate Income With Your Land

THE BIG STOCK MARKET

No, I am not talking about the New York Stock Exchange big board but the big-time live(stock) market. For most homesteaders this means cows, but it could mean bison, water buffalo, or large flocks of sheep. I will put pigs in there as well. It goes without saying that you will need adequate pasture land to accommodate these voracious grazers, and that there are many benefits to raising them. For example, if you purchase a young bull for $1,000 or so and five ready-to-breed heifers for the same price, your $6,000 investment will likely produce five calves that will be fed for free (by their mothers and your pastures) each year for 12 to 15 years.

What will you do with these calves? Perhaps you will sell them as stockers when they are weaned, or perhaps you will raise and market grass-fed beef, which I will discuss in chapter four. However, to give you a sneak preview, if you were to raise the calves as grass-fed beef, it is likely that, given current prices, each calf would become worth approximately $2,000 for you (net) in about two years if you sell them to urban markets. These prices are rising steadily, which is in your favor, but clearly there is a ramp-up period of a couple of years before you realize any income. Once the cows are ready for market beginning in year three, those five heifers will be throwing off about $10,000 per year in gross profit ($2,000 per calf X five per year). If they do this for 12 years, then your initial investment of $6,000 for the bull and heifers will return a gross profit of $120,000. Try getting those returns in the stock market.

Staying with this scenario and assuming each cow needs one acre of grazing land, you will need approximately 16 acres of pasture. This is for, A) the initial bull and five cows (6), B) the five calves born the first year that will take two years to grow (5), and C) the five calves born the second year (5). After the second year the five grown calves will be sold or processed, clearing the way for the five new calves born the third year, keeping the pasture demand static at 16 acres. Now, there are entire books on this topic, such as *Grass-Fed Cattle: How to Produce and Market Natural Beef,* and I encourage you to read them if this path interests you.

Grass-fed beef and lamb

Of course, generating these returns requires that you purchase land for the animals. While the chart below shows the national average value of pasture land to be $1,200 per acre, good luck finding that in most areas. In my neck of the woods, pasture land goes for $3,000 to $5,500 per acre, which is probably a better average to work with for most new homesteaders. So, the 16 acres of land necessary for grazing will cost anywhere from $48,000 to $88,000 (not to mention paying modest taxes on the land), which takes a big "capital" bite out of the gross profit. I emphasize the word "capital" because the land acquisition cost does not reduce your profit since, if you desired, you could sell the land at the end of the 12 years, likely get back at least what you paid for it and still have earned the $120,000. Plus you would still have a dozen or so cows left over. Purchasing land ties up your capital for a LONG time, which is why you are entitled to the returns you can generate through certain farming enterprises. The returns go along with the risk and loss of capital.

2013 Pasture values and lease rates[1]

Region/State	Pasture value				Cash rent ($/acre)		
	2013 value ($/acre)	1-year change (%)	3-year change (%)	5-year change (%)	2013 rent ($/acre)	1-year change (%)	Rent income yield (%)
Northeast:	**3,270**	**1.2**	**1.9**	**-6.0**	**30.50**	**1.7**	**0.9**
Maryland[5]					39.50	-1.3	
New Jersey	13,400	-0.7	-3.6	-18.8	28.00	7.7	0.2
New York	1,240	-0.8	3.3	12.7	17.50	2.9	1.4
Pennsylvania	2,700	3.8	3.8	-12.9	35.00	-7.9	1.3
Vermont[5]					23.00	4.5	
Other states[2,5]	5,810	0.5	1.0	-8.8			
Lake States:	**2,020**	**8.0**	**12.2**	**9.8**	**30.50**	**8.9**	**1.5**
Michigan	2,700	8.9	8.0	2.7	26.00	4.0	1.0
Minnesota	1,750	16.7	25.0	18.2	28.00	14.3	1.6
Wisconsin	2,150	0.9	2.9	8.9	35.00	2.9	1.6
Corn Belt:	**2,490**	**9.2**	**18.6**	**19.1**	**35.50**	**7.6**	**1.4**
Illinois	3,700	19.4	32.1	45.1	53.00	51.4	1.4
Indiana	2,700	3.8	8.0	7.6	37.00	-11.9	1.4
Iowa	3,400	13.3	28.3	64.3	49.00	6.5	1.4
Missouri	1,950	7.1	14.7	8.3	29.00	3.6	1.5
Ohio	3,300	3.1	10.0	3.1	25.00	-16.7	0.8
Northern Plains:	**816**	**18.4**	**46.8**	**58.1**	**18.50**	**12.1**	**2.3**
Kansas	1,250	25.0	54.3	66.7	17.50	6.1	1.4
Nebraska	700	6.1	32.1	45.8	20.00	14.3	2.9
North Dakota	630	28.6	53.7	80.0	15.00	7.1	2.4
South Dakota	710	20.3	51.1	51.1	20.00	14.3	2.8
Appalachian:	**3,410**	**4.3**	**3.3**	**-5.8**	**22.00**	**2.3**	**0.6**
Kentucky	2,800	12.0	15.7	8.9	27.00	8.0	1.0
North Carolina	4,750	5.6	0.4	-2.5	26.00	0.0	0.5
Tennessee	3,600	0.6	0.0	-7.2	20.00	0.0	0.6
Virginia	4,150	1.2	-1.2	-14.1	21.00	0.0	0.5
West Virginia	2,150	2.4	2.4	10.3	12.00	9.1	0.6
Southeast:	**3,380**	**-1.5**	**-8.4**	**-32.9**	**18.50**	**12.1**	**0.5**
Alabama	1,600	3.2	0.0	-11.1	20.00	5.3	1.3
Florida	4,200	-2.3	6.7	-29.2	16.00	28.0	0.4
Georgia	4,200	0.0	-16.0	-43.6	24.00	0.0	0.6
South Carolina	2,700	-5.3	-6.9	10.0	18.00	12.5	0.7
Delta States:	**2,270**	**3.7**	**4.6**	**5.1**	**17.00**	**-2.9**	**0.7**
Arkansas	2,400	4.3	4.3	9.1	18.00	0.0	0.8
Louisiana	2,400	4.3	9.1	16.5	15.00	-16.7	0.6
Mississippi	1,950	1.0	1.0	-11.4	17.00	6.3	0.9
Southern Plains:	**1,520**	**2.0**	**7.0**	**13.4**	**7.60**	**1.3**	**0.5**
Oklahoma	1,330	15.7	27.9	33.0	12.00	4.3	0.9
Texas	1,560	0.0	4.0	11.4	6.50	0.0	0.4
Mountain:	**558**	**1.3**	**6.3**	**-9.6**	**5.00**	**0.0**	**0.9**
Arizona[3,5]					2.00	-9.1	
Colorado	680	6.3	6.3	4.2	4.60	0.0	0.7
Idaho	1,210	0.0	-6.8	-24.8	13.00	18.2	1.1
Montana	580	1.8	9.4	23.7	6.00	1.7	1.0
Nevada[3,5]					14.00	16.7	
New Mexico[3]	350	0.0	12.9	12.9	2.80	0.0	0.8
Utah[3]	950	3.3	3.3	1.1	6.00	20.0	0.6
Wyoming	440	-2.2	2.3	8.3	4.50	6.3	1.0
Pacific:	**1,680**	**1.2**	**4.0**	**-11.6**	**13.00**	**4.0**	**0.8**
California	2,800	0.0	0.0	-7.3	12.00	4.3	0.4
Oregon	680	9.7	1.5	-8.1	18.00	-14.3	2.6
Washington	820	1.2	0.0	6.5	11.00	22.2	1.3
National average[4]	**1,200**	**4.3**	**9.1**	**10.1**	**12.00**	**4.3**	**1.0**

[1]Land value estimates are as of Jan. 1 for each calendar year and are based on the National Agricultural Statistics Service June Area Survey, conducted during the first two weeks of June. Data for cash-rent rates is collected via survey from mid-February to July. Land rented for a share of the crop, on a fee per head, per pound of gain, by animal unit month (AUM), rented free of charge, or land that includes buildings such as barns are excluded from the survey. [2]Other states includes CT, DE, ME, MD, MA, NH, RI and VT. [3]Excludes American Indian reservation land. [4]Excludes Alaska and Hawaii. [5]Land values and cash-rent rates for some states is not published due to insufficient data and/or high variability of individual state data. Rent income Yield: Gross rent divided by land value; excludes property taxes, insurance and other landowner expenses.

Source: Farmland Investor Letter analysis of USDA data

Do you have to own land to raise livestock? No you do not, and some farmers follow Missouri farmer Greg Judy's advice in his book *No Risk Ranching*. Today, Judy runs a grazing operation of over 1,400 acres of LEASED land over 11 farms. He and his wife went from near bankruptcy in 1999 to paying off a 200-acre farm within three years using his custom grazing model. Using the above example of starting modestly with one bull and five heifers, you could consider leasing pasture land adjacent or local to you for perhaps $30 per acre, per year. Your annual rent would be $480 for 16 acres and you would have no income from the grass-fed beef operation to offset this for the first two years. However, after this you would generate $10,000 per year in income, far more than you would need to cover the expenses. In this model, however, you would need to lease land that had good water (which will cost you more) or incur the cost of drilling a well. You would also have to fence it, as Greg describes in his book, but you would tie up far less capital. Perhaps you can even be debt free!

You may incur other minor expenses such as hay when grass is not growing, vet bills if you plan to use vets, and, of course, taxes on the land you own, but the income will drastically exceed the expenses... IF... you can market the product successfully. For more on that, see the section in chapter six on marketing your homestead products.

I caution you to avoid exotic animals unless economic times are very good or are likely to be. In poor economic times, people want and need basic foodstuffs and materials, and your attempt to market grass-fed zebra may prove more challenging than you expect.

You can do similar calculations to scale this up or down, or with other species such as pigs, bison, and so on. The point is this: putting the animals to work allows you to generate a stream of FUTURE income, improve your soil, and create wealth. The wealth is held not necessarily in fiat currency but in the value of your fertile soil and livestock.

**Bottom line? There is big income potential with large
livestock, but it requires a lot of land and the confidence to
handle large animals.**

THE SMALL STOCK MARKET

You guessed it… I am not talking about you becoming the Gordon
Gekko of the pink sheets but rather raising rabbits, goats, chickens,
turkeys, eggs, bees, and the like on a limited scale. These species are
much more common on the homestead than water buffalo and herds
of grass-fed cattle, and for good reason. They are smaller, easier to
handle, and, in many cases, you can even process (slaughter) them
right on your farm or homestead and sell to consumers, which you
cannot legally do with red meat (lamb, pork, and beef).

No doubt that many, if not most, of these small livestock belong
on every homestead, but keep in mind there is a difference between
you raising rabbits for YOUR meat and you raising meat rabbits
to generate income. Unlike the example with the cows, you will
need to continually purchase feed for rabbits (and especially
chickens) and the cost of feed can vary widely from year to year
with commodity price swings, making it difficult for you to plan.
The amount of income you can generate is rather limited if your
goal is to be a farmer, but may easily help to sustain a homesteader.

For instance, if a single doe produces four litters per year of eight
kits each, we will assume you may have 30 fryers to sell (losing two
to mortality) each year at a weight of three pounds each. If you
could charge $6 per pound, then each doe would generate $540 in
sales of rabbit meat before subtracting feed costs. Alas, you would
better be prepared to butcher them yourself as your beef processor
might be a bit perplexed if you hauled in a load of rabbits for
slaughter. Multiplying this by 10 does, for example, brings your
sales to $5,400; 30 does drives sales to over $15,000. Of course, in

the latter example, you now have 900 butchered rabbits to sell, so be prepared for that.

Alternatively, you could consider breeding heritage breed animals and selling the babies to consumers. Many people are looking to purchase specific breeds of rabbits, chickens, turkeys, pigs, sheep and goats. If this appeals to you, look into what initial breeding stock can be purchased for and how much animals are selling for today in your area. This way you can get your animal husbandry "fix" without having to butcher as many animals. In my area, weaned meat rabbits can be sold for $10 each for the more common New Zealand Whites to $25 each or more for more rare heritage breeds, such as the American Chinchilla. Similarly, chicks of laying breed varieties are often sold for $10 to $15 each, especially for breeds such as the Ameraucana.

The author, his wife and their laying hens

If small livestock is more interesting to you than the large animals, you may want to consider having multiple species. It is not hard to imagine someone visiting your farmstead to purchase a few of your point-of-lay (POL) laying hens for $15 each, but then plunking down more cash when they see you have:

- Day-old heritage turkey poults,
- Baby lambs and breeding-age sheep,
- Pygmy goats,
- Livestock guardian dogs.

Small stock could also include honeybees, which may be particularly attractive with all the concern about colony collapse disorder. With bees you can sell nucs, full hives, two- or three-pound bags of bees or just queens. For many commercial beekeepers, this is quite a lucrative endeavor!

Bottom line? Small is beautiful, but smaller the livestock, the smaller the absolute income potential.

FARM STAYS, EVENTS, WEDDINGS, & PRIVATE PARTIES

Agritourism has been an area of constant interest, and I expect this to continue even if economic conditions are soft, for it is not only YOU who is being called to the land. We are all becoming more aware of how disconnected we are from our natural world, a problem exacerbated daily as each old pasture morphs in the night to become a morning sub-division or parking lot.

Can you not imagine a soon-to-be-married couple wanting to have their wedding overlooking your beautiful pastures, ponds, and happy animals? I can, and they will pay well for it, because competitive alternatives also charge good money for the service. But ask yourself if this is a one-time, seasonal or continuous opportunity? Perhaps it is seasonal at best depending on how well you market it, but getting back to re-purposing all your investments and efforts, you could use the same facilities for corporate retreats and other events.

What about a farm-stay bed and breakfast in your home or in a refurbished barn? Sounds quaint, romantic, and what a lot of people would be in the mood for, does it not? If you do not want to use your house, you can always provide a glamour camping (glamping) experience instead. It could be a yurt, tee pee or the wall tents that are offered at Mary Jane's Farm bed and breakfast… for $240 per night. Remember that when economic conditions are soft, they are not necessarily soft for everyone, as wealthy folks generally do just fine and retain plenty of disposable income. Mary Jane's Farm is not the only one catering to these well-to-do customers. The Martyn House, an 18-acre restored homestead just over an hour north of Atlanta, offers upscale glamping in wall tents as well as event facility rentals, farm dinners, a bed and breakfast, and weddings. Heck, they will even rent the entire farm if someone wants it!

A wall tent at Mary Jane's Farm

If these ideas are too upscale for you, then consider setting up a permanent tent camping area and facilities on your land. Jinny Cleland did just that at Four Springs Farm on her Vermont farm, where she also offers event rentals, baked goods, catering, poultry, fruits, vegetables, and much more.

If you do not want guests staying overnight, then you could consider farm dinners. These outings normally feature local chefs and offer the advantage of introducing paying customers to other products or services you have available. For example, Green Dirt Farm in Missouri has a series of farm dinners and cheese appreciation events throughout the year. The cheese appreciation events are $50 per person and the 11 farm dinners per year, limited to 30 people each, all sell out at a price of $170 per person. That works out to $5,100 in revenue per dinner, or just over $56,000 per year just for the dinners. The cheese appreciation events can generate another $15,000 in sales. To be sure, there are expenses to offset this for food, chefs, and marketing, but this is a very nice ancillary business to their main business of producing fantastic farmstead sheep's milk cheese. Of course, their location being only 30 minutes from Kansas City ensures they have a base of customers to whom they can market, as well as chefs upon whom they can rely, but the point is for you to consider proximity to markets before you purchase land if this is something that interests you.

Variations - RV/tent farm camping, summer youth farm camps, pond fishing, corn mazes, Easter egg hunts in the spring, haunted woods in the fall, etc.

A farm dinner at Nature's Harmony Farm

SKILLS CLASSES

To an extent this belongs in the agritourism category as well, but the emphasis is on teaching skills to consumers. What skills? How about cheesemaking, butchering, hide tanning, traditional survival skills, foraging, soap making... you name it. For example, butchering classes can run the gamut from this $50 hog-butchering class

The author leading a hog butchering class

on a Wisconsin farm all the way to Fleisher's $10,000 butchering class that may have to be reserved a year in advance!

Other ideas include offering traditional survival skills, such as the ones offered by Earth School, SurvivalSchool.com, Mountain Shepherd Wilderness Survival School and many others. Demand for these classes are constantly increasing. Are they available in your area? If not, could you offer and market them, even if you had to hire expertise to deliver? If you have or are searching for a smaller homestead near a major market, could you use that as a platform to teach lucrative skills classes rather than relying on more "traditional" homesteading products for income? Just a thought.

I know what some of you are thinking. *Sure, this works for others, but I do not have the skills to offer classes.* If that is the case, fret not, for all you have to do is commit yourself to learning. After all consider that a few years ago I had never made cheese, but it did not take too long to achieve enough competence to teach others to do so, and many others have done the same. You just have to uncover your passion, practice and master your art, and then share your passion with others.

The idea of offering educational skills classes seems to be an area that many homesteaders and farms ignore. Perhaps they feel they do not possess the patience or demeanor to meet consumer expectations. If you are comfortable with students or people in general, then consider offering skills classes. It will do far more than generate seasonal or continual income for you; it will forge a bond with many of your visitors that will motivate them to become loyal supporters of your homestead. Classes have the added benefit of not tying you permanently to the farm (unlike animal husbandry), since you could concentrate the classes in specific months and free other months up for chores… or a vacation back to the city. :-)

I have briefly mentioned classes in this chapter because, in some cases, land is required to teach the classes (such as animal husbandry, primitive skills, etc.). This is not always the case, of course, so for many more ideas on classes, see the next chapter, Make Money With Your Skills.

BECOME A GROWER

This is why you want to become a homesteader, right? To put your hands in fluffy soil, tug gorgeous carrots right out of the ground, cut fresh flowers that you planted, snip asparagus in early April… If these iconic images of homesteading inspire you, then it is reasonable to expect consumers will want the same. Retreating to my earlier mention of one-time, seasonal or continual-income opportunities, "growing" is one income area that can absolutely be as year-round as you want it to be. And, unlike farm stays or classes, eating is not normally viewed as a discretionary expense. After all, people gotta eat and I will go out on a limb and predict that will never change.

If you are considering homesteading or farming, I suspect you already know that growing is one of your income options. The growing options range from growing veggies throughout the year to seasonal fruits to fresh flowers, herbs, and even exotics—things that normally are not locally available. Think dried tea leaves, bananas, and oranges from your greenhouse, etc. Unlike livestock, exotic fruits would likely do quite well.

Because growing food is at the heart of being a homesteader or farmer, you will find there are many others who want to grow too, and you will find yourself in (hopefully) friendly competition with them for a share of the consumer's wallet. It is a given that your produce must be healthy, delicious, and gorgeous, but you will also benefit from being a savvy marketer if you expect to get your share of the market. Funny thing, that… you do not see many marketing books on the homesteader's shelf, I suspect. Am I wrong in that assumption, or does modern homesteading not also mean applying modern small-business savvy to the business of homesteading?

There are lots of great books on growing, including several by Eliot Coleman that I highly recommend. Just remember that if you are new to gardening and if your garden plot is new, you should expect it to take at least three to five years before your soil tilth and fertility catches up with your expectations of light and fluffy soil.

To summarize this opportunity, it is natural that you may want to be a market gardener, and there should be a growing appetite (could not resist) for organic fruits and vegetables. But do not think it is necessarily so easy to, A) be a good grower, B) convince mother nature to always cooperate, C) gain access to good farmers markets, and D) get product to customers before it spoils. Take it seriously and plan for success if it is success you hope to achieve.

Variations - Mushroom cultivation, selling live plants, greenhouse transplants, heirloom seeds…

PROFILE # 4

"I felt like an imposter, using up my life doing work I did not care about or enjoy."

– Keith Stewart

Who: Keith Stewart, Farmer and Author

Where: Western Orange County, NY. Born and grew up in New Zealand

Homestead/Farm Highlights: Was a dairy farm until my wife and I purchased the property 28 years ago when it became an organic vegetable and herb farm. Has 88 acres divided between cropland, pasture, and woods. A creek runs through the farm and there are three ponds. We have a house, a dairy barn, pole barns, workshop and worker housing.

What was your "real job" prior to breaking away to become more self-sufficient? Project manager for a real estate consulting firm. Before that, I worked with an engineering consulting firm and was involved in site selection and relocation studies for large companies. Before that I was a school teacher and laborer in London, UK, and drove a cab in New York City.

What inspired (or scared) you into wanting to be more self-sufficient? My heart was not in the corporate world. I felt like an imposter, using up my life doing work I did not care about or enjoy.

When (if) you left your "real job" in suburbia, what was the most challenging thing about taking the leap to your new life? Learning how to farm profitably.

What inspired you to become a grower? I wanted to work outside with nature in a healthy environment, to be my own boss and make my own decisions for better or worse. To use my body as well as my mind.

What are your sources of income? Vegetable and herb sales at a farmers market in New York City. Plus some modest income from writing.

Do you sell mainly directly to consumers or to restaurants/distributors? Why did you choose that sales path? I sell directly to consumers and chefs, and am a big fan of the full retail dollar. Interacting with the public at an urban farmers market is a nice change from working on the farm.

How did you come to be an author and write *It's a Long Road to a Tomato?* I dabbled in writing without much success through most of my life. About 16 years ago was invited to write an article about local farming for the first issue of a new magazine (the Valley Table) focusing on food and local agriculture in the Hudson Valley. I hesitated for a day or two, then said okay, knowing that writing is hard work and that I already had a very full plate. The next night I sharpened my pencils, rolled up my sleeves and went to work. A month later I submitted a 1,000-word piece. The editor was happy with it and asked for another. Before long I was given my own "locally grown" column. I've written for almost every issue of the Valley Table magazine since then. It's a quarterly, so just four times a year.

After several years, a publisher in New York City showed up at our farmers market stand, said he had read several of my pieces and asked if I would be interested in doing a book. Thus *It's a Long Road to a Tomato* was born.

About five years ago an acquiring editor at Storey Publishing who was familiar with *It's a Long Road to a Tomato* asked if I would be interested in doing a book for them — a comprehensive how-to for beginning and relatively new organic farmers. Again, with some amount of apprehension, I said yes. Writing this new book, *Storey's Guide to Growing Organic Vegetables and Herbs for Market* — all 560 pages of it over a two-year period — was probably the most challenging thing I have ever done.

If you left a "real job" in suburbia, what was the most challenging thing about taking the leap to your new life? Making do with less income for several years and learning the farmer's trade were the biggest challenges. But, since I was enjoying myself so much, I did not really mind.

Starting a business for the first time can be scary. Do you have a marketing background? I had some knowledge of marketing, though not strictly a marketing background. The Greenmarket in NY City is a tremendous outlet for farmers. If you can consistently grow good food, treat your customers well, and learn how to run a business, you have a fair chance of success.

If starting over, what would you do differently? I might try working for other farmers for a year or two before taking the plunge.

What do you miss about city/urban life...you know, the "real" world? My life bridges the two worlds — rural and urban — and I like them both, though temperamentally I am more at home on the land. Suburbia leaves me cold.

What advice do you have for someone considering leaving a "real job" to become more self-sufficient? Read the first 30-odd pages of my book, *Storey's Guide to Growing Organic Vegetables and Herbs for Market* or, more specifically, Chapter 1, "Thinking About Becoming a Farmer" and Chapter 2, "Looking for a Place of Your Own." If that is too much to ask, immerse yourself in the world of local and sustainable agriculture before you take the leap. Go to organic and local farming conferences, read books and publications like Growing for Market, talk to farmers, network with others with similar goals. Seek out successful farmers who are doing what you want to do and, if at all possible, spend one or more seasons working for them. Before starting out on your own, the more knowledge and hands-on experience you have, the better.

FARMSTEAD CHEESE AND/OR RAW MILK

Ah, here we go… the great raw milk debate. Well, it is not my intent to delve into whether it is permissible or not to sell raw milk. If this is an opportunity that you are interested in, then it is your job to find out the regulations and follow them strictly, but it may be well worth your time to do so. Milk prices in general are at all-time highs, and prices for raw milk currently range from $5 to $15 a gallon across the country. Moreover, with fluid milk, cash flow is immediate, as you can get paid almost before the cow misses the milk. In contrast, you will not be paid for some aged cheeses for a year or longer after the milking!

So why are there not more farmers selling raw milk and making cheese? If you look around you, wherever you are, you will observe far more farmers and homesteaders selling vegetables and produce than selling milk. And, you will find more dairies selling fluid milk than those who make and sell cheese. This is because it takes more time, cash flow, capital, risk assumption and know-how to produce and sell cheese than it does to produce milk. The fact is, there is a correlation between profit margin potential and risk (or barriers to entry) in any business, including farming. Naturally it costs far more to set up a Grade-A farmstead cheese operation than it does to build a dozen chicken tractors or set up a few raised beds, and the corresponding profit margin potential is commensurate with that increased risk and investment, making this an attractive opportunity if you are prepared to make the financial and intellectual investment.

I can tell you from personal experience that cheesemaking is a fun, intellectual, and very rewarding pursuit. I can also tell you that, compared to other farming enterprises I discuss in this book, it is the most capital intensive—at least if you are interested in farmstead cheese, in which case you own and milk the animals. On the other hand, the sheer capital nature of the cheese business along with the intellectual property of the cheese recipes and aging procedures creates a

Farmstead cheese and Jersey cows at Nature's Harmony Farm

natural barrier to many who would like to join the industry… and compete against you.

Of course, you do not have to go the farmstead cheese route. You can produce wonderful artisanal cheese by purchasing milk from other dairies if they are close to you. If you have not moved yet and believe this may interest you, research the location of possible dairies, visit with them and, if all goes well, use the location as a guide to where to look for your own land. For an example of this, see the profile on Looking Glass Creamery in the Artisan Cheese section of chapter four.

Whether you choose the farmstead or artisanal cheese path, you must then decide between pasteurized or raw milk. One financial benefit of pasteurization is that you can sell cheeses at a much younger age (immediately, in fact), whereas with raw-milk cheeses the requirement (for now) is that you will have to age the cheese for 60 days. This means that with raw milk, you are looking at making blues, semi-firm, and firm cheeses rather than the chèvre, soft mozzarella, brie, and camembert so many love. Moreover, with soft cheeses, more of the milk turns into cheese, resulting in yields as high as 15 percent or more since the cheeses include over 50 percent water (consumers do not seem to mind).

Now compare that to aged cheeses. In my case, one cheese that I have made a great deal of is called Fortsonia, a firm cheese modeled after Gruyere. Fortsonia averages only a nine percent yield, which

The author and his wife, Liz, making farmstead cheese

equates to another financial benefit of pasteurization, since without that process and with the increasing FDA pressure on soft, raw-milk cheeses, I am forced to make low-moisture cheeses. A final financial benefit of pasteurization relates to cash flow, for it allows cheesemakers to sell cheeses as soon as they produce them, if they would like.

For milk, your options include goats, sheep or cows. Cows require the largest investment, both in terms of grazing land as well as larger milking and handling facilities. Then again, if you want to be an artisan cheesemaker rather than a homestead cheesemaker, you could simply buy milk from a local dairy and set up a commercial cheese operation. If you want to become a cheesemaker, I strongly recommend you consider going this route to start, but you will likely be limited to cow milk. Finding sufficient quantities of goat—and especially sheep—milk to purchase for artisan cheese production can be a challenge. You can always add your own animals to milk in the future but this path allows you to minimize risk and focus on just getting the cheese "right" rather than dealing with all the headaches of animal husbandry. And making cheese is only half the battle. You have to sell it, meaning you will have to hone those marketing skills even more.

Variations - butter, yogurt, cream, buttermilk, ice cream (all require pasteurization)…

SELL SOME GRASS

Sure, marijuana is becoming increasingly legal, but that is not what I am referring to. Rather, if you find yourself with some decent pasture acreage, you can use it in many ways to create a "cash crop," but the ideas I have in mind will not make Cheech and Chong too proud. I am thinking of custom grazing or selling organic hay.

Custom grazing is a contractual arrangement where you provide the pastures, fencing, water, and grazing management for others who place their animals on your land. You can charge either by the day, by the pounds gained or both. If you are short on cash but long on time and enthusiasm, this may be a good option for you.

Let us say you had 40 acres and you wanted to improve the fertility anyway. You may strike a deal to graze 40 cows, stockers or cow/ calf pairs and someone else would provide the animals that you would not have to pay for. Be careful if you take in bulls, as they will eat 50 percent more, on average, than cows so your stocking rates (and the prices you charge) need to reflect this.

In a stocking scenario, you may have 40 weaned calves dropped off in April that you allow to graze until October. Let us assume they arrive weighing 550 pounds each and your pastures could allow them to gain two pounds per day on average for 180 days. By the end of October, each stocker would weigh 910 pounds, having gained 360 pounds (180 days X 2/lb/day). In total, you would have added 14,400 pounds of beef (180 days X 2/lb/day X 40 head). If you charged a rate of $.60 per pound of gain, then your income for the six-month grazing contract would be $8,640. Rates vary, of course, and you could charge much more in drought/ dry areas than in lush areas. Then again, you would achieve more weight gain in lush areas than you would in dry. Believe it or not, you do not even need to own land to custom graze for others. You can lease land close to you if you have a smaller homestead and do not have the room yourself.

Another alternative for some income is to produce organic hay, either for the grass-fed beef or horse quality market. By the way, organic does not just mean letting your pastures go... it means having quality forages that are non-GMO and managed organically with no chemicals at all. You will get more per ton for square bales than round, but those in the cattle market will very likely not want to fool with square bales, so you should choose your market first. If you do not own hay equipment, then you can hire out the job, but this is often challenging since all hay tends to come in around the same time and those with hay equipment are in pretty good demand during those times.

Variations - Blend marketable tree plantings into grazing areas to form a silvopasture, thereby generating both current income from grazing and long-term income from timber.

BREED AND BOARD

Do you love animals and desire to become a breeder? There are many ways you can do this on your homestead. Of course you can use the large or small livestock mentioned above and become a breeder of rabbits, sheep, goats, pigs, cows or any combination. There are always ads on Craigslist and in local agriculture publications for these and many people look to buy weaned piglets, 4H rabbits and calves, and so on.

Another idea is to breed and train livestock handling or guardian dogs, such as shepherds or collies to herd sheep and cows, or Great Pyrenees to protect livestock. I expect both of these to be in constant demand as more and more preppers and homesteaders emerge and need proven genetics to help with their animals.

The author with one of his heritage Ossabaw pigs

If you love horses and your new homestead has a barn of sorts, offering boarding and grazing for horses may be just the thing for you. You may be able to charge $150 to 250 per month or trade in value for full 24/7 pasture turn out. The more you can offer, the more you can charge, but of course, rates vary from region to region. It is yet another way you can generate income from a homestead parcel that you could not from a city apartment.

If you are in a good traffic area or close to larger markets, an alternative is opening a doggy day care (pet-sitting service) or even a full-fledged kennel.

LEASE LAND TO HUNTERS

Two trends will converge to continually drive up the lease price for hunting land, in my opinion. The first is that rural land continues to be absorbed by developers and private land owners, resulting in less land available for hunters. The second is that, along with population growth, more and more people are being called to the land in one way or another, and one of those ways is to have land to hunt. Many hunters have the deep desire to hunt with their children and pass on skills they value, but they often live in the city, work "normal" jobs and need a place to escape to. If you find yourself with a sizable piece of good hunting land and are not inspired by the more labor-intensive farming ideas presented in this book, consider leasing the land for hunting. It will not generate enough income to sustain you, but combined with other income sources it could prove to be the key ingredient in your recipe for financial success on the homestead.

FIREWOOD AND BASIC MATERIALS

Finally, you are sitting on a gold mine of sorts with your new piece of land. You will likely have woods that could offer rough timber, firewood, and pine straw, among other things. If you are handy with a chainsaw or if you want to invest a few thousand dollars in a portable sawmill, you could be producing lots of custom-cut lumber.

Understandably, many people look upon all the rocks on their land disapprovingly, but these rocks and boulders could become landscape rocks for someone else, particularly if you are close to an urban market. Although this falls more into the one-time income-stream category than continual income, it could be a good way to clean up your land while beautifying another person's property at the same time!

PROFILE # 5

Hummingbird-
use the blade to cut and aerate the soil.

> "The "real" world is knowing, helping, and getting help from your relatives and neighbors."
>
> – Jo Ann Holdredge

Who: Randy and Jo Ann Holdredge,

HoldredgeEnterprises.com

Where: Central New York State

What was/is your "real job" prior to becoming more self-sufficient?: Randy was an Electronics Design Engineer.

What inspired/scared you into starting down the road to becoming more self-sufficient: Moving back to the family farm from California after Randy's father passed away.

Homestead/Farm Highlights: Randy is the fourth generation to live on the farm. It was a working dairy farm until the early 60s. Now, the larger fields are rented to a local dairy farmer for growing crops. Our gardens occupy the smaller spaces.

What are your income streams?: We are starting a small family company to manufacture a garden tool that Randy invented. We are also restarting a garlic business.

Do you homestead full time or part time, and why?: I do not think we would be considered true homesteaders. We have chickens for our own eggs and grow various vegetables for our own use as well as selling at our small farm stand.

How and why did you develop the Hooke 'n Crooke?: Coming from California where we discovered that we LOVE Mexican food, we wanted to grow our own garlic. Weeding the garlic was a BIG problem. There were many tools on the farm, but none seemed to do an adequate job. Randy's history as a Design Engineer led him to start developing the Hooke 'n Crooke. He knew he could design a better tool.

When he finalized the design, he knew other gardeners would appreciate a tool that worked as well as this one. It is quite different from anything on the market. Once people see it in action and can use it, they are amazed at all it can do and how well it works, with less effort. As we say, it almost makes weeding fun.

Starting a business like that for the first time can be scary. How did you market your tools?: We were naïve. We knew we had a great product and so of course, we called one of the larger garden-tool manufacturers to see if they would be interested in licensing or manufacturing the tool. They did not actually laugh at us, but what were they to think? Along comes this guy out of the blue saying he has a great new tool. Little did they know of Randy's design background as well as his early life on the farm. When things break on the farm, generally you fix them yourself. A farmer makes do with what he has and his own knowledge. We started out on a very minuscule financial base. We first contacted various magazines to see if they would put the Hooke 'n Crooke in the New Products sections. Next, we placed a few small ads in other magazines. We started attending festivals as a vendor. We found that word of mouth is our best sales technique. We are a small company with steady, slow growth.

If starting over again on the path to self-sufficiency, what would you do differently?: Most likely nothing. With the very generous help from family and friends we are doing things ourselves. We get input from neighbors, customers, family, and friends. We have applied for a patent. Someone once told me, "More is not always a good thing." Growing too fast could cause problems. Right now we are doing things ourselves. We know this tool can go nationwide. We are coming to the point where we will be looking for help. When the patent is granted, we will be in a better position to approach large tool manufacturers.

What do you miss about city/urban life…you know, the "real" world?: The "real" world is our rural life, here on the farm. You might find turkeys outside your bedroom window. The deer leave tracks through your pea patch where they just had breakfast. The roosters start crowing at 4:00 a.m. You take in a stray cat and all of a sudden, as if by magic, you have 12 cats. The "real" world is knowing, helping, and getting help from your relatives and neighbors. When something breaks down, you fix it. If you can envision a better, easier way to plant garlic, you create the machine that does it. You do not go to the movies and stay out till 10:00 p.m. You stay out until 10 rolling the winter rye that you just finished planting to catch the rain that the weatherman says is coming tomorrow.

When we lived in Southern California, we really enjoyed it, but our "real life" is being back on the farm.

What advice do you have for someone considering leaving a "real job" to become more self-sufficient?: The terms "real world" and "real job" have different meanings for each of us. Truly know what kind of person you are. Have the support group (spouse, children, relatives, friends) that you will most certainly need at some point. Be prepared for hard work and long hours, with the possibility of a small amount of financial gain. Your reward will not come with the purchase of a new car or a nice vacation. Your satisfaction will come in seeing the first hint of your crops coming up in the spring. Watching the geese getting into formation for their long trip south will replace going to the movies. Worrying about paying the bills will replace worrying about being robbed at the local mall. Hearing acorns falling on the roof will replace the sound of police sirens. Truly know who you are and what you are willing to accept and what rewards you are looking for in your search to find your own happiness.

While some ideas in this chapter touch on product offerings, the above represent just some of the ways you can use your land to generate income. Some techniques are quite passive and very long term (silvopasture) while others are very labor intensive and offer immediate income gratification (transplants). Some require a lot of capital and appeal to those aiming for a larger business while others require only a modest investment for those dreaming of a truly simple life. Of course there are more ideas, but this is enough to get you thinking.

Knowing how much money you need to earn, how much capital you are comfortable risking and, most importantly, what you are passionate about, you will find the ideas that are right for you. But remember:

Saving Money = Making Money!

To a homesteader's way of thinking, you not only save money and therefore need to earn less (and therefore pay less in taxes) by producing so much yourself, you also lock in prices and create a personal buffer from inflation. Milk prices may go through the roof for everyone else (and indeed they are at an all-time high as I am writing this), but yours will always be the same. So while the ideas expressed above focus on generating income, remember that you will be reducing your costs at the same time as you transition from a consumption household to a production household.

Chapter Three
Make Money With Your Skills

"Teaching kids how to feed themselves and how to live in a community responsibly is the center of an education."
— Alice Waters

Whoever you are, I am confident in assuming one thing about you: you have one or more skills. I have never met someone who has none, though I have met many who were unaware they had any. And your roster of skills and capabilities will only expand when you move to the homestead as you learn all sorts of new gardening, farming, mechanical, crafting and other talents that others desire to learn and are willing to pay for. The trick for you will be to market those skills into income-generating assignments that will allow you to comfortably live your dream life off the land.

I hope the previous chapter gave you ideas about how your land could work to generate income for you, and the next chapter will give you numerous ideas for products you can sell. This chapter offers a rapid-fire listing of money-making ideas that bridge the gap between your current/future skills and market opportunities. Almost all these ideas I have either used to generate income myself or have paid my fellow rural compatriots to provide services to me. Some of the ideas are physical and must be performed locally while others can be performed from anywhere with Internet access and sold to consumers around the world. The ideas are presented briefly since, in some examples, there are entire books devoted to their application and opportunity. This list, therefore, is intended to stoke your cerebral fire and get you to visualize what appeals to you. I hope you will pick a few ideas and take the opportunity to further research them as you personalize your farmstead business plan (see chapter six).

So what is the difference between skills and products? Essentially it boils down to products being tangible in themselves with skills being talents, knowledge, and capabilities that are not themselves tangible. Rather, they can be employed to fulfill a need or desire, tangible or not.

If you have hay to sell, that is a product (as a result of your skill operating hay equipment) and I will focus on that in the next section. If you have knowledge to produce far more hay than average due to your understanding of pasture management, that is a skill and perhaps you could earn money consulting with that knowledge.

In this chapter I will focus on skills and services you can sell as a farmsteader and I will divide the list into two macro categories. The first will involve physical skills for tasks you can perform for your local community. You need to be in close proximity to your customer to make money with the ideas on this list. The second will involve virtual/online skills for services you can easily sell to anyone around the world and collect money via PayPal, digital currency, check or wire-transfer.

If you are interested in an idea below but do not have the skills yet, just remember that it is not too late. You will be learning LOTS of new skills as a homesteader. Once you earn the knowledge and training necessary, you can start earning income with it.

Ready? Let us begin!

PHYSICAL/LOCAL SERVICE IDEAS TO MAKE MONEY HOMESTEADING

GENERAL SERVICES

Folks in rural areas have many "general" needs. By the way, just because you are moving "out there" to become more self-sufficient does not mean that the people already there think that way. You may be surprised to learn they value the convenience of grocery stores and having hired help to do things for them. What things?

- Fence installation and repair,
- Automatic gate installation and repair,
- Painting,
- Household repair (Mr. Fix It),
- and so on.

If you are interested in or handy with any of these, then put the word out by printing a business card and pinning it at the local feed store and elsewhere where people congregate. Be sure to join the local Chamber of Commerce.

TRACTOR WORK

One way to really justify (or rationalize) the purchase of a tractor and its implements is to use it not only for your property but to hire it out for local projects. The jobs you can hire it for depend on the tractor's features (does it have a front-end loader, for example) and the attachments you have. Depending on the equipment, you could earn good income by:

- Cutting/baling hay,
- Mowing large fields,

- Disking,
- Tilling,
- No-till drilling,
- Seeding/planting (if you have a tractor but not a planter, you can often rent a seed drill or planter locally and still provide the service),
- Maintaining long gravel driveways and/or snow removal,
- Bush hogging,
- Moving piles of dirt/gravel/debris and more.

Advertise yourself for free on Craigslist and at local stores such as feed stores, hardware stores, coffee shops, and grocery stores.

GARDENING WORK

I expect you will become expert at organic gardening and growing food in no time. If you believe everyone in the country grows their own food, let me assure you that is a myth. Most country folks have lost the skills to grow and preserve food along with the rest of society, so do not be shocked when you find that others are happy to depend solely on the grocery chains for sustenance. At best, a few folks may have only a summer garden, but more often than not, it relies on chemical controls and tilling.

More and more people are likely to become interested in organic and no-till methods of growing food and you can profit from this trend by "marketing" your expertise to others. What can you do?

- Install raised beds or drip irrigation lines,
- Set up compost bins,
- Set up or show them how to capture rainwater for the garden,

Get the idea? There is A LOT you will be learning that others will not know but will want (and need) to know.

TEACH PERMACULTURE CLASSES

These classes allow you to practice what you live. Presumably you are moving to a more self-sufficient lifestyle to effectively produce more of your own food and learn life-sustaining skills that would otherwise be lost. Before embarking on your homesteading journey, you may read Sepp Holzer's innovative book on *Hügelkultur* and create your own Hügelkultur beds. Or perhaps you will read *Gaia's Garden* or create your own forest garden. If you do, then you will have the perfect platform from which to teach others how to do the same! After all, if you wanted to learn this, then so do others. Here are just a few ideas you can start with:

- Teach them how to build soil with manure/leaves/grass clippings, garden without tilling, schedule successive plantings and winter gardens, and protect plants from frost,

- Teach them how to companion plant or how to trap plant for pests, etc.,

- Teach them how you set up your aquaponics garden (you did, did you not?),

- Install Hügelkultur beds (if you are unfamiliar with Hügelkultur, research this fascinating way to grow food with a low-maintenance, no-watering method),

- Show them the food forest you created (you did create one, did you not?) on your new homestead and teach them the method!

TEACH PREPAREDNESS CLASSES

National Geographic sensationalized dozens of families who are seeking self-sufficiency in their program Doomsday Preppers, and the show was very popular for a reason. Just look at the popularity on Amazon of numerous "how-to" books such as *How to Survive the End of the World as We Know It* by James Wesley Rawles, *Prepper's Long-Term Survival Guide* by Jim Cobb, and literally hundreds of other titles. Even the fiction category is besieged with doomsday scenarios that rank high on the best-sellers list, including no fewer than eight books in the *Holding Their Own* series by Joe Nobody. Laugh at your peril, but this topic has been high on the Amazon sales chart in recent years and interest is climbing rather than waning.

So what does this mean for you? You will be learning many preparedness skills as you embark on your homesteading journey, even if you do not fully realize that yet. It is true that many preparedness courses seem to focus on wilderness or survival skills, but remember, we are interested in modern homesteading. Perhaps you can reach out to those who are interested in learning to be more prepared rather than learning how to make a fire out of wet leaves. For example:

- Teach food preservation (when to dehydrate, when to pressure can, etc.) after you learn and practice it,
- Teach food storage (when to use five-gallon buckets and mylar, when to use dehydrated food, how to source, store, rotate, etc.),
- How and why to create bug-out bags,
- How and why to create get-home travel bags,

For inspiration in this area, consider Jill Winger, founder and owner of ThePrairieHomestead.com. Jill has not only created a wonderful blog on all things homesteading that is effectively monetized, but she has also authored numerous books. Let me share her story with you.

PROFILE # 6

"It has been the most fulfilling life-change I have ever made."
– Jill Winger

Who: Jill Winger, Author and owner of ThePrairieHomestead.com blog

Where: SE Wyoming

If you left a "real job" prior to breaking away to become more self-sufficient, what was it? I worked as an assistant horse trainer and also as a vet tech before quitting my jobs to become a stay-at-home mom. Having more time at home as a mom enabled me to pursue my passions of self-sufficient living.

Homestead/Farm Highlights: We bought our 67-acre chunk of prairie in 2008. It was in bad shape and had previously been a neglected rental property. We saw potential in it, but it took five years of blood, sweat, and tears to get it in the state it is in now. The house was built in 1910, and is small and boxy. Part of the reason this property appealed to us is because of the outbuildings; it came with a barn, shop, and chicken coop. However, they required a lot of work before they were usable again. Since purchasing our property, we have repainted, re-fenced, resided, and re-roofed all the buildings and have also hauled away thousands of pounds of trash and planted many trees.

What inspired (or scared) you into pursuing a more self-sufficient lifestyle? It was a rather strange conversion for me, since I had been a girl who just did not care much about natural "stuff." We originally wanted our property to have room for our horses, but even before we signed the papers to make it officially "ours," a plan started developing in my mind, and I started thinking of things I never had before: composting, chickens, dairy animals, and gardening. Once I had this vision of becoming self-sufficient, it became an all-consuming desire, and I have not looked back since. It has been the most fulfilling life-change I have ever made.

What were your criteria when looking for land? How did you make your choice? We knew we wanted more than the five-acre plots that are typical in our area. We needed enough land to keep our horses and also potentially some cattle. Outbuildings were also a must-have, since our winters are long and cold and we needed at least a temporary shelter for our existing animals while we planned out our projects. We also considered trees, water availability, and mineral rights– all criteria that our current property fulfilled, at least partially.

What are your income streams now? My husband has maintained a job "in town" as an electrician throughout this whole process (although that will likely be changing soon, as he is planning to quit his job to begin helping me with my businesses). My blog brings in steady revenue each month. However, our largest income stream is a home business (essential oils) I started several years ago as a part of the network-marketing industry. It has allowed us to create a team that spans all over the globe and currently is our largest income stream.

On your blog you mention following Dave Ramsey's method for debt management. How did that help you to realize your dreams of homesteading? Before we married, we made the commitment to stay debt-free (other than a mortgage), thanks to Dave Ramsey's advice. Hands-down, this has been the best decision we ever made. We have always lived within our means, and although it has meant driving older vehicles and often having to fix or borrow old equipment, it set a very important foundation for us. Now, as our income has grown, we have been able to funnel that income into projects and investments. We are also getting closer to having our mortgage completely eliminated.

Starting a website (blog or otherwise) can be intimidating to people who are not used to that sort of thing. What tips have you learned about monetizing blogs that you can share with other "wannabe" homesteaders who may be interested in this avenue?

1) **Be patient–** It can take years to develop a platform that brings decent income. However, do not let that scare you away– the time will pass anyway.

2) **Stay consistent–** Post consistently. Success online generally equates to lots of small efforts over a period of time.

3) **Have multiple income streams—**Do not put all your eggs in one basket. Diversify your income plan to ensure you stay stable, regardless of the Internet's ever-changing whims.

If starting over again on the path to self-sufficiency, what would you do differently? Many things! Our biggest lessons have been:

1) **Plan it first!** We have had to re-do many projects due to poor planning at the beginning...

2) **Use quality materials to start—do not skimp**. Our extreme penny-pinching ways early in our marriage worked against

us a bit. We used to think that the cheaper the material, the better. However, after being forced to re-do several projects after the materials either broke, fell apart, or disintegrated, we have learned the value of investing in quality up-front. It saves time, money, and headache.

3) **Dream bigger**– I hate to admit it, but we thought small when we first started. Those limiting beliefs worked against us, until we learned how to dream bigger for the future.

If relevant, what do you miss about city/urban life...you know, the "real" world? Not much! Every time I go to town, I find myself becoming increasingly thankful for our rural life. However, I will admit there are times being able to run to the grocery store for a quick supper ingredient would be nice.

Finally, what advice do you have for someone considering leaving a "real job" to become more self-sufficient? Do not be afraid to begin building your dream while you are working the "real job" to support it. Remember, this lifestyle is a learning process, so there will be good days and bad days—embrace them all and never, ever give up!

ORGANIZE CLASSES AND EVENTS ON TOPICS YOU CANNOT TEACH, BUT CAN MARKET

Perhaps you are interested in teaching classes, but there is a problem; you do not yet have the skills to teach a subject. What do you do? Simply hire (or better yet, barter with) someone to do it with you. That is how we offered our first whole-hog butchering class on our farm. We had a professional butcher teach the class and we were able to learn alongside others who wanted to learn the skill. After that class and spending another year practicing at home, we were able to offer charcuterie classes ourselves and teach customers how to make their own dry-cured meats such as pepperoni, salami and so on. It was even more popular than the butchering class and since we also raised pigs, customers bought pork at the same time so they could practice their new skills once they returned home.

What kind of classes could you offer via a partnership? Here are a few ideas:

- Wilderness survival with a survivalist
- Foraging with a foraging expert
- Emergency medical care with experts
- Butchering classes with a butcher
- Cheesemaking classes with a consultant

Believe me, there is a growing interest in these and many other related topics. After all, you are not the only one reading this and similar books. While you may be interested in taking the leap to self-sufficiency, the vast majority of people will never be able (or courageous) enough to do so. Still, they will look to live vicariously through someone like yourself, so fund your homesteading dreams by giving them the fulfillment they long for.

GUNSMITH SERVICES

Are you mechanically inclined? Do you have experience or a passion for gunsmithing? If so, there is no reason why you cannot do basic repairs or modifications in your local area from home. Remember, though, that working on guns is only one part of the equation. The bigger part is embracing that you are NOT a gunsmith. Rather, you are running a gunsmith BUSINESS. This means dealing with licensing (FFL, etc.), marketing, keeping books, etc. I mention this necessity here, but it applies to all ideas in this book. If this idea interests you, consider a course at a gunsmithing school.

LOCKSMITHING SERVICES

Our friends made the leap from urban life to rural homesteading a few years back and embraced numerous income-producing strategies. In addition to selling eggs, animal treats and small livestock, they used their knowledge to create a locksmith service, something that was lacking in the area. So you see, there are many ways you can approach earning income while living a much more self-sufficient life in the country.

CUSTOM KNIFE MAKING

Good custom knife makers can earn attractive incomes making and selling custom knives. If you have the talent, tools and materials, you too can live your homesteading dream from making and selling knives.

SHARPENING

Similar to knife making, sharpening knives, chainsaws, and tools is a skill you could learn expertise in. You will likely need to do these things for yourself anyway, so why not make some extra bucks by offering the service to others? After all, hairdressers, farmers, and chefs all depend on sharp cutting instruments. Often, they pay professionals to sharpen their blades for them.

TEACH HERBALISM

Many people have embraced medicinal herbs and more traditional healing. Most homesteaders dabble in foraging and growing some herbs, but you can go beyond a cursory interest and turn it into an income-producing passion, just as Robin McGee did in South Carolina.

PROFILE # 7

"People are hungry for
this knowledge."

– Robin McGee

Who: Robin McGee. I live with my husband on his family's farm…
Double M Farm, Inc. Our website is carolinagrassfedbeef.com. The
original acreage came to his family via a land grant from the King of
England back in the 1800s. My actual plot is 2 acres and includes
my home (build in the 1800s), gardens, huge old oak trees, and the
old "car house" building that will serve as a classroom.

Where: Anderson, SC in the middle of a 500-acre farm.

**If you had a "real job" prior to breaking away to become more
self-sufficient, what was it that you left?** It was more like I had
jobs "out there," because it is what is expected. I tried to find joy
in several areas. The most rewarding was doing floral design (for
a locally owned business, then a major corporation, and then for
myself as a contractor for weddings and events)…creating beauty
from beauty to send love and light into other's lives. I decided to
be a stay-at-home mom when I had my last child. Now, THAT is
a REAL job!

The last "out there in the land of delusion" job I had was as executive assistant to the president of a multi-national corporation that specialized in art and educational materials for early childhood. I was a glorified customer service agent whose job was to lie to customers and kiss the ass of the company's owner.

What inspired (or scared) you into pursuing a more self-sufficient lifestyle? I have always been an "I will do it myself" kind of girl, so it is always been part of who I am to be self-sufficient.

To further my desire of living sustainably and self-reliant is the lack of common sense displayed by our society and our government. I read labels. If I cannot grow it in my yard or a greenhouse then it is not edible, so why would I put that in my body? How is it that it is ok for the regulators to slowly poison us? To poison Gaia and all of her inhabitants? We, and our planet, are treated like commodities.

I do not want negative energy infused into my work whether it be gardening, harvesting, wildcrafting, making plant medicine, or preparing for a class, and I do not want to send more negative energy out into the universe. I am a firm believer that everything we do effects the whole, and I would rather be responsible for raising the vibration of the planet, for sending love and light out into the universe.

I no longer choose to participate in perpetuating the insanity. I do not watch TV, I do not have a family doctor, I do not have insurance, I do not eat their poisons, and I do not take their drugs. I do not want to be distracted anymore by the illusion. It makes more sense to me to look for peace, joy, happiness, abundance, love, and magic…the invisible threads that connect us all to what is really real—to remind people that we are more powerful than we have been led to believe.

Homestead/Farm Highlights: So many micro-habitats. Mixed hardwood forest, hay fields, pastures, creeks, 2 ponds, gardens (veggie, culinary & medicinal herbs, At-Risk medicinal, and a mountain garden), basically a Botanical Sanctuary, a little swampy area, and we border Lake Hartwell for several miles. White Oak (my absolute favorite Tree and favorite medicine), Red Oak, Post Oak, several species of Pine and Hickory, Sweet Gum, Tulip Poplar, Holly, Hop Hornbeam, Black Haw are some of the trees. The biggest patch (football field-size) of naturally occurring Bloodroot I have ever seen. Soooo many wild edibles and medicinals (plants and fungi).

What are your income streams? Herbs, classes, products, etc. I teach classes on wild-crafting, plant ID, plant energetics, Doctrine of Signatures, herbal first aid, remembering the magic, tree medicine, herbs for babies and children, how to make herbal tinctures, salves, syrups, oils, and soaps, how to can and ferment foods, etc., and I lead plant walks, teach at conferences and events, and sell herbal products, also do a few private consultations, and am a frequent guest speaker for plant, homesteading, gardening, groups. My husband raises grass-fed, grass-finished beef, and free-range eggs. (carolinagrassfedbeef.com)

Why did you choose teaching workshops as an income route? It filled a great need in the Upstate of SC...someone HAD to do it! For the sake of the people, the plants, and knowledge, and the heritage! I did not go into this with the intention of it become a source of income....that just happened. People are hungry for this knowledge. It is my calling...to be a bridge between plants and people, to help people remember who they are and their birthright, to empower them, and to honor the plants.

How did you acquire the knowledge (and confidence) to teach your herb classes? Confidence...hahaha! I have confidence in the Green World. I am just doing what I was born to do, and I have never been afraid of public speaking, of stating my views, my own truths, and it is important for me to share the stories of the plants. I have always been connected to Mother Earth, Gaia, nature.

I remember as a little girl watching TV with my daddy, you know, those old westerns and nature shows. The characters I most related to were the American Indian Medicine Man and the old herb woman in the woods. I could not become an Indian Medicine Man, but the old herb woman…that was something I could be! I have always had gardens and gardening books. I began searching for herbal medicine classes in my area and found no classes and no schools anywhere in my area teaching herbal medicine. NOT ONE! I finally found an online school and took their Family Herbalist Certification program. The school hosted an annual Natural Healing Conference. I attended two of them while doing the program. The first plant walk I ever attended was led by Darryl Patton. I never had met anybody who knew so much about the plants that grow around me, how to use them for food and medicine, how the old timers and the Indians used them. A few other teachers at those conferences were Matthew Wood, David Winston, Rosemary Gladstar, David Hoffmann. Matthew Wood became my teacher, my mentor, my friend. I attended week-long workshops with Matthew, which led to me meeting other teachers who became relevant in my learning and growth, like Kathleen Maier, Phyllis Light, and Kate Gilday. And as grateful as I am to these amazing teachers, it is the plants and trees who continue to be my greatest teachers. I am in such awe of these amazing green allies, and I want everyone who feels the call to learn how to use these plants and trees and fungi that grow around us for food and medicine. I am a Lorax!

Starting a business for the first-time can be scary. How did you market your workshops to get customers? Do you have a marketing background? I did not really start out with the idea of what I do being a business. It is just what I do, and who

I am. That people are willing to pay to learn how to do what I do or to listen to me talk about plants and trees is a bonus. Go to where the people are you are trying to reach. For me, that meant alternative health stores. I spent many hours hanging out with the owners, listening to the stories of their customers, and eventually, as my herbal studies continued, the owners began to ask ME what I would recommend for this ailment for that person. I began making my own herbal medicines early on, so I had stories of how well they worked from using them with my family and friends. Word of mouth is great advertising. It also meant farm-type festivals… folks who live closer to the land usually want to know how to do things naturally. I always took a "Sign Up for Class Info" sheet to get email addresses of interested folks. Now I use Facebook to share classes and workshops.

If starting over again on the path to self-sufficiency, what would you do differently? I believe that everything is right on time. The distractions of the matrix, the land of delusion, must have been necessary. It got me where I am, this place of knowing who I am and why I am here, honoring this dance called life

If relevant, what do you miss about city/urban life…you know, the "real" world? NOT ONE DAMN THING!

Finally, what advice do you have for someone considering leaving a "real job" to become more self-sufficient? To paraphrase Thoreau, "Go confidently in the direction of your dreams. Live the life you have imagined." Align yourself with what you want. Your energetic vibration must match the energetic vibration of what you desire. Be specific. Words are powerful, so pay attention to what you put out there.

Take care of yourself FIRST! We have been taught that we should always put others first.

RV REPAIR

Repairing recreational vehicles is not necessarily overly difficult, but it is specialized. Given the concerns about the economy, jobs, and so on, it is reasonable to anticipate there will be more and more people taking economical RV getaways or simply living in their RVs. This means more people will need repairs and, let us face it, how many RV repair people do you see on the side of the road? This is an opportunity to specialize and become "the" RV repair person for your area. I have a neighbor who has done just this. His house near a main road allows him to generate a constant stream of income repairing RVs while keeping a valuable self-sufficient skill finely honed!

MECHANIC

If you are good at mechanical repair then people will need your help. It is always hard to find a good mechanic. If you are also good at small engine repair and farm equipment repair (tractors, RVs), then you will be even more in demand.

START A CSA OR FOOD CO-OP

Some farmers struggle with marketing and distribution, but perhaps this is an area you are good at. If so, consider becoming a distributor for local farmers and getting their products to retailers, restaurants, resorts, and other stores. It will be good for the producer, good for the buyer, good for the local community and you will not have to produce anything yourself!

PROFILE # 8

"If you are planning on selling at markets, first become a buyer at those markets."

– Eric Wagoner

Who: Eric Wagoner, Athens Locally Grown,

Locallygrown.net

Where: Athens, GA

If you had a "real job" prior to breaking away to become more self-sufficient, what was it that you left? I have got a regular 9 to 5 office job that I have had ever since I moved to Athens in 1997. It is pretty much an ideal environment for me, with flexibility, insurance, places to exercise my creative and technical skills, and so on. I had thought I would have transitioned away from this to homesteading full time long before now, and if I worked anyplace else, I probably would have.

Homestead/Farm Highlights: I was lucky enough to stumble on a motivated seller of thirteen acres with a long stretch of frontage on the Broad River. It was cheap, secluded, had a house and a workshop already on it, and seemed like an great place to start up a life of self-sufficiency. There was no garden, orchard, or anything like that already there, so I knew I was going to have to put all that in myself. The terrain left very little space suitable for working with a tractor, so the gardening would have to be done on a small scale, by hand. That is my favorite way to garden, though, so that was ok by me.

What inspired (or scared) you into pursuing a more self-sufficient lifestyle? I have always had a garden, since I was a child, and my parents and grandparents were also gardeners and farmers. I have always lived in the country or small towns — Athens is by far the largest community I have ever lived in. Working in the dirt is a source of comfort and a chance to meditate. Being able to provide for myself is also a key personality trait of mine, and homesteading naturally ties all that together.

How did you fund your homestead dreams...was debt a problem? Even though the land was cheap it was still at the edge of what we could afford. I wanted the land to be able to pay for itself as quickly as it could, and that meant jumpstarting the gardens so we could begin selling at the farmers markets the very first season we were there. With our savings depleted on the mortgage down payment we did turn to borrowing for truckloads of compost, lumber to build a chicken coop and garden shed, tools and seeds, market equipment, and so on. It was a lot of money to borrow, but we did make it back eventually.

What are your income streams? When the homestead was at its peak, money came in through the sale of vegetables, eggs from our small flock of 100 hens, fruit from wild blackberries, and foraged products (sumac, herbs, etc.). We also made fresh pestos from garden items, grew sprouts and micro greens, and similar items, but constantly changing state regulations eventually put and end to those streams.

Meanwhile, I kept my office job, even though the commute became 40 minutes each way after we moved to the farm. I also took on occasional software development and website consulting work.

How did you get the idea to start locallygrown.net? Our first season growing for market, 2002, the existing growers at the small organic Saturday market in Athens were looking for a way to sell their items mid-week. They decided to adapt the concept behind an existing state-wide cooperative of growers that sold to chefs in Atlanta and scale it down to just Athens. I was invited in as one of the founding members, and we hashed out the logistics for doing that. We decided I would build a web front-end for the group to list our products and take orders from chefs, and that was the first iteration of locallygrown. We called ourselves Athens Locally Grown Cooperative (though we were not a true co-op), and decided we would open up to our regular Saturday customers as well as restaurateurs. I built the system largely with open source e-commerce tools and added to or re-wrote parts of it as we moved forward. After the first two years, the farming couple who ran the day-to-day side of things gave that part to me, and I have been running it all ever since. We grew to become (for a time) the largest farmers market in the southeast.

Locallygrown.net is licensed to operators across the country. How did you get the idea for that vision and what skills were required for you to execute on it? As far as I can tell, ALG was the world's first virtual farmers market. I started to get invited out to conferences to talk about what we had put together, including SSAWG in New Orleans and the Kerr Center in Oklahoma. In my presentations, I walked though all the open source tools I had used to put the market together, the business end behind it, and how they could build something similar in their communities. As it turned out, though, the skill combination I had (software and website development, vegetable production, and marketing) was much rarer at the time than I thought, and no one I talked to was able to re-create what I had done on their own. Finally, in 2006 I decided to take the year off from farming and spend that time plus any other hours I could scrape together and completely re-write the system and turn it into a turn-key hosted platform for communities anywhere to use. In January 2007 I turned on the lights, and now there are hundreds of markets across North America using the system.

Even with my software and website experience, I had to learn a lot along the way. I had to learn or get better at server management, database design, accounting and business management, graphic design, marketing, writing, and more to pull it off. In the end, the project succeeded, and now other market managers can create or bring their existing markets online without having to learn all those skills themselves.

Starting a business for the first time can be scary. How did you build your customer base? Do you have a marketing background? I do not have a marketing background myself, but I have worked in small business where we all wore many hats and I have had to work closely with those who had marketing backgrounds. I am a firm believer that if you provide a good product and a great customer experience, your customers will do your marketing for you. That has been largely true. I have also been afraid, especially in the early years, that we would grow faster than the growers could grow vegetables, and then we would lose all those customers because we could not feed them. So, I never advertised or did a traditional marketing campaign so we did not get a flood of curious people who would leave disappointed. The natural growth via word of mouth just naturally matched the growth our farmers could keep up with.

If starting over again on the path to self-sufficiency, what would you do differently? I do not know if I would do anything differently. Over the long term, for a number of reasons unrelated to homesteading, having a farm did not work out for me and I am now back in town. I did underestimate how much time and effort my partner and I would need to put into growing crops, especially after health issues arose (and of course after having a couple children). When I do eventually start over (and I have no doubts I will), I will take that lesson into account. Even though I am off the farm now, I still run the market and stay involved in the community of growers. Perhaps I would start on a much smaller parcel, a couple acres at most, so I could be much closer to town.

While homesteading, what did you miss about city/urban life... you know, the "real" world? The commute was the worst. It was an easy drive, and gave me time to listen to podcasts, fiction, and music, but it ate up 90 minutes of the day that I could not use for anything else. Living out of town was also very isolating, and I missed communal dinners, game nights, and general getting together with friends. The gathering we did have tended to be larger and more involved, because we were in a sense making up for all the day-to-day interactions that had fallen away. Living only 20 minutes out of town instead of 40 would have made a huge difference, but we had to look far afield to find something we could afford with the acreage we thought we needed.

Finally, what advice do you have for someone considering leaving a "real job" to become more self-sufficient? Start small. A half-acre garden is huge when you are doing it intensively and by hand, but when you are starting out it is tempting to jump on a tractor and till up several acres to put in row crops. I have seen so many people do that, and it is easy at first but soon becomes completely overwhelming. Also, if you are planning on selling at markets, first become a buyer at those markets. Get to know the other growers, what they grow, how they grow it. Learn from them — market growers who do not want to share their knowledge are few and far between. I have seen a number of growers who suddenly arrive at a market with bushels and bushels of squash, without doing any of the preparatory legwork, going home again with bushels and bushels of squash.

WELDING

Many people in rural areas know how to weld but most do it for themselves or their farm. The opportunity is there to offer welding and small fabrication for hire, if this is a skill you possess.

SHEARING

If you have sheep on your homestead you could shear them yourself and then hire this service out to others. Most sheep owners do not shear themselves and it is always hard to find someone local who does.

A/I

No, not artificial intelligence but rather artificial insemination (A/I). With more and more homesteaders and small farmers starting up with smaller herds of animals, many do not want the danger or cost of having bulls, boars, and rams on their property. Or perhaps they simply want to add genetic diversity to their herd by using A/I. Either way, if you learn this skill and make the modest investments in equipment, then you will be in demand for sure. As an example, there is no one remotely in my area who offers this, I am sad to say. There is an unfulfilled need for this service in many areas.

BOARDING

Earlier, I mentioned how boarding could be an offering that your land could enable, but you could expand this if you are skilled with horses by offering riding lessons and horse training. There are horse people in every neck of the woods, so you would likely find a waiting clientele.

EQUIPMENT OPERATOR

Perhaps you do not have the equipment to hire out but you do know how to operate a tractor, bobcat, bulldozer, track loader, excavator, ditch witch, backhoe or the like. There is always a need for this in the country. In fact, when I had 50 acres to clear, I purchased a used bulldozer but hired an experienced operator to do much of the clearing when I did not have the time. That operator could have been you!

CARPENTRY

If you enjoy building, then you are in luck as this is a skill that most people either do not have or do not have time for. From repairing buildings to constructing sheds, additions, barns, and so on, you will probably find more work than you can handle as fewer new homes are built and more repairs/add ons are in demand. And, to broaden your offering even more, learn and then teach cob building techniques!

ELECTRICIAN, PLUMBER

If you are skilled and licensed, people will need these services. If you develop skills with alternative energy and plumbing techniques, such as setting up solar well pumps, you will be able to charge a premium!

HAULING ANIMALS

You may have a truck and purchased a livestock trailer when you moved to the country. Guess what? Not everyone has one. Let locals know you can haul livestock for them or post your skill on Craigslist. As with many ideas here, this should not be seen as a full-time job, but it could be combined with many other jobs to round out the income you need.

PHOTOGRAPHY

With fancy new phones anyone can take a picture. However, only skilled photographers can compose and create an emotive work of art worthy of celebration… and compensation. If this is one of your talents, then you will have a unique income stream. Check out sites such as istockphoto.com and shutterstock.com and learn how you can get paid for high quality photos you take.

COMPUTER REPAIR

Are you good with computers and Internet issues? Many people are not, particularly in rural America where you hope to live. If you are good with eradicating viruses, freeing up memory, recovering files, providing Internet access alternatives and the like, then you are in luck… and in demand!

WILDERNESS SURVIVAL COURSES

As mentioned earlier, wilderness and preparedness survival training has become extremely popular. If you have not yet mastered these skills, companies such as Sigma III Survival School will teach you expert survival training so you can open your own school. How exciting is that!?

One expert in the field who is already doing this is Richard Cleveland, founder of Earth School, profiled below.

PROFILE # 9

> "If you do not know how to forage, hunt, or fish you are ultimately a dependent liability."
>
> – Richard Cleveland

Who: Richard Cleveland

Where: Western North Carolina

What: Earth School (lovetheearth.com)

Were you always a homesteader, or did you leave a "real job" prior to breaking away to become more self-sufficient? I grew up in a commercial family painting business in the Chicago suburbs. I was never drawn or led, by fear, to a self-sufficient lifestyle. I felt a deep connection to nature from a very young age. I am really not sure, but as I witnessed the urban sprawl that was happening all around my area, I certainly started to question our rich farmlands being turned into cookie-cutter neighborhoods and mega-malls. It just did not feel right. Something in my bones, even back then, told me that this was not sustainable.

Homestead/Farm Highlights: I own no land currently and honestly, as I witness the current economy, I am thankful I do not have a mortgage. I live on a large organic farm and enjoy tremendous biodiversity. To me the perfect marriage is incorporating responsible farming/homesteading with wild-crafting... something all our ancestors shared.

What are your income streams? I generate income mainly by my programs. Teaching people how to take care of themselves is not only satisfying but the main focus of my school. Reconnecting people to their ancestral roots and wisdom is empowering and I believe, paramount to a self-sufficient lifestyle.

Why did you choose teaching classes as an income route over more traditional products? Quite simply, teaching people the skills to take care of themselves eliminates their dependency on others for their survival. It fosters and creates an environment for them to barter their goods and services and ultimately create real sustainable communities.

How did you acquire the knowledge (and confidence) to teach your classes at Earth School? I owe a lot to Tom Brown Jr, honestly. He opened my eyes to "what I was missing in nature." I was a full-time instructor at his school from 1993 to 1998. Other teachers/mentors include David Winston, Charles Worsham, Dr. Errett Callahan, Scott Silsby and Jack Cresson. From that time up until now I have literally taught these valuable skills to tens of thousands of people.

Starting a business for the first time can be scary. How did you market your classes and products to get customers? Do you have a marketing background? Marketing is everything to a business! However, it is a double-edged sword... it takes money to make money... not always an easy thing for new businesses. I certainly have experienced and do experience this paradox.

If starting over again on the path to self-sufficiency, what would you do differently? Aside from marrying into a rich family...

nothing! :) Seriously, the choice of living a self-sufficient lifestyle has its financial challenges, but I am content with the choices I have made. I feel pretty blessed to be able to make a modest living teaching people about nature's many gifts.

If relevant, what do you miss about city/urban life...you know, the "real" world? Honestly, I do not miss anything about my suburban past. A Native American mentor referred to society (AKA "Real World") as an illusion. He said... "Anything that cannot sustain itself without destroying itself is temporary and therefore an illusion." Do not get me wrong... I love people, but I do feel that our society needs to re-connect with nature on an intimate scale. Leaving this Earth a better place for generations of children we will never meet is our responsibility...

What advice do you have for someone considering leaving a "real job" to become more self-sufficient? Simply... you cannot be self-sufficient without knowledge! A "real job" means being dependent on the system. Real self-sufficiency is being able to provide for yourself. If you do not know how to forage, hunt, or fish you are ultimately a dependent liability! You and your loved ones would benefit greatly from you reversing that "reality."

GUIDED FISHING OR HUNTING SERVICE

Talk about a job you can enjoy long into retirement, how about offering services as a fishing guide! Of course, this is after you have made a considerable investment in the area and art of fishing it. Before you begin, consider offering yourself as a free guide to friends to see how it goes. Be sure NOT to put your line in the water, as that turns your attention to fishing, rather than guiding and coaching. As a fishing guide, your job is to create a lasting memory for a group of buddies, fathers and sons, mothers and

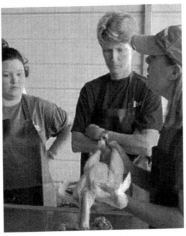

A chicken butchering class at Nature's Harmony Farm

daughters, and families. Do it right and you will enjoy it as much as they do.

Alternatively, if you have land (or access to land) but are reluctant to sell hunting leases, you could offer guided hunting trips to generate income and still retain control over access to your property.

TEACH MEAT PROCESSING

Now, you cannot do this as an inspected processor unless you want to go through the red tape process, but since you will likely learn how to skin rabbits, eviscerate chickens and maybe even slaughter sheep and goats, you could offer this as a service for others who want to butcher their own animals. Just be very careful how you position this; you are selling ONLY your knowledge and service and in no way are you selling meat, since the animals already belong to the customer.

ONLINE/VIRTUAL SERVICES TO MAKE MONEY AS A HOMESTEADER

EARN MONEY ONLINE

As I have mentioned, I do not know you or what specific skills you have. That said, there are LOTS of ways to make money online using skills you probably already have. I do not want to define each of these here, so let me just list a few ideas for you to think about or research:

- Copy editing
- Freelance and content writing of e-books, articles, blog post, press releases, product reviews, proof reading, forum posts...
- Illustrating for authors, web designers, etc.
- Become a Virtual Assistant (VA)
- Offer research assistance to authors, editors, and writers
- Web or graphic design
- Web security consulting
- Voice-overs
- Language translation

If you have talent in any of these areas, freelancing can afford you the ability to earn income from the comfort of your homestead. Generally it requires a decent Internet connection, so add that to your list of criteria when finalizing your location. If you have a background in writing, administrative support, legal services, graphic design, programming, illustration, and many other areas, freelancing can be a great option.

Not sure how to find these opportunities or how to market yourself? Try eLance, Guru, Sideskills, Fiverr, or iFreelance. You will probably be surprised how many opportunities there are as you explore the listings and categories. Pay can vary from just a few dollars to several thousand depending on the job requirements and duration. I have first-hand experience with hiring freelancers as, over the past 15 years, I have hired dozens of proofreaders, editors, graphic designers, illustrators, SEO specialists and more myself for various business and book projects. These sites offer tremendous advantages to hiring managers and represent a great income opportunity for you. Just be sure to specialize, earn GREAT reviews and differentiate yourself, otherwise you will likely get lost among the other freelancers.

Another option is Tutor.com which, if you are qualified, allows you to earn income by offering online tutoring.

There are many examples in this book of homesteaders who are earning a living online, in one way or another. A great example follows of a couple who are carving out a living with books, blogs and farm products that they sell online. Meet Mark Hamilton and Anna Hess.

PROFILE # 10

"If I could go back in time, I would take the plunge to financial self-sufficiency sooner."

– Anna Hess

Who: Mark Hamilton and Anna Hess (waldeneffect.org)

Where: Southwest Virginia

What: We homestead on 58 acres of swamp and hillside, but we only actively manage about two acres of the land for food production. We grow most of our own food, although we still buy some meat and fruit.

Were you always a homesteader, or did you leave a "real job" prior to breaking away to become more self-sufficient? Mark had several "real jobs" before we moved to the land, while I got by with part-time jobs that allowed me to work on my homesteading skills in the extra hours.

What inspired (or scared) you into wanting to be more self-sufficient? My parents were back-to-the-landers in the 1970s and 1980s, and they dragged me away from the farm at just the right age — when I had had time to taste the joy of homesteading life, but had not been forced to participate in any of the work. I yearned to find my own farm ever since moving to town in fourth grade.

Mark was more of a city boy, although his parents' roots were in rural Kentucky. Although he had not dreamed of homesteading before meeting me, he always wanted to find a way to leave the rat race and to have more time for creative pursuits.

If you left a "real job" in suburbia, what was the most challenging thing about taking the leap to your new life? The biggest challenge from a financial perspective was thinking through the whole year, rather than depending on a weekly paycheck. We had to plan ahead for the waxing and waning cycle of annual sales, filling up our savings account as a buffer against the lean seasons.

What are your income streams? For several years after taking the plunge into self-sufficiency, our primary income came from selling the chicken waterers that Mark invented (www.avianaquamiser.com). However, over the last few years, writing has become a larger and larger proportion of our income, with my self-published books (www.wetknee.com) bringing in the most revenue but with some income from a traditional publisher also. Finally, we receive a small but significant income from ads and affiliate sales from our homesteading blog at www.waldeneffect.org.

If starting over, what would you do differently? We kept working off the farm for a few years after moving to our homestead, which was stressful since the jobs left us with less time than we really needed for farm tasks. If I could go back in time, I would take the plunge to financial self-sufficiency sooner.

What do you miss about city/urban life… you know, the "real" world? Mark most misses the easy social contact that the urban life provided. He lived in Albuquerque for quite a while before moving back east, and finds it much harder now to hook up with like-minded people. Anna never really lived in the "real world", so she cannot comment.

> **What advice do you have for someone considering leaving a "real job" to become more self-sufficient?** It is a leap of faith, and you have to be brave, but the harvest will be worth it.

CONSULTING

What do you do today? Is it something in business, academia, law, medicine, technology, etc. that you could offer as a distant consulting service? Can you package it into an online or remote training offering? Perhaps you are an accountant and setting up and managing Quickbooks is easy for you, but challenging for folks around you. Or maybe you are a business hot shot with expertise in logistics, marketing, human resources or strategic planning. With all those skills I bet you can figure out how to offer business coaching, life coaching, or consulting online.

START (AND MONETIZE) A BLOG

Blogging has proven for many to be an effective tool for income generation, whether full or part time. In fact, in this book alone I profile numerous people who have turned their passion for self-sufficient life into money-making blogs, including Rural Revolution, The Walden Effect and more.

AUTHORING

Many authors, including Wendell Berry, Gene Logsdon, James Wesley Rawles, Joel Salatin, myself and many others have relied on publishing as a dependable source of income earned while living their rural dreams. Could you be the next one? Why not?

If you have solid writing skills and can identify the right topic for the right audience, it is easier than ever to publish and, more importantly, distribute print books with print on demand (POD) offerings from Createspace by Amazon, Lightning Source and others. Just take a page out of other authors' books and remember the importance of BRANDING yourself and your expertise. If you offer great content and develop a following as they have, loyal readers will eagerly purchase your next book and you will be on your way to a long-lasting passive income stream.

If this area interests you, however, please consider this: While it is true that Amazon makes it easier than ever for new authors to get their words in front of reader's eyes, this ease of publication places much responsibility squarely upon the author; responsibility that formerly was shouldered by the publishing house. This includes cover design, grammar, proofreading, editing, titling, tightening copy, editing again, and so on. If you hope to succeed as an author rather than simply writing a book, you must accept the burden of ensuring these critical responsibilities are addressed so your words are presented to readers as clearly and concisely as possible.

Do not let these tasks intimidate you. Rather, embrace them. After all, is not taking personal responsibility for so much consistent with the overall mindset of homesteading? Do not let these diverse tasks overwhelm you and get help where you need it. Just as you may aspire to earn money online, be prepared to pay others to do proofreading and design for you. Be sure to find and work with exceptional people if you aim to produce exceptional work.

MONETIZED PODCASTING

I cannot tell you how many different podcast shows and episodes I have listened to over the past few years. Needless to say, the number is in the many thousands; like many of us, I seek greater control over what I feed my brain. Before moving to the homestead we listened to and were inspired by podcasts on homesteading and farming. Now that I am here I find myself listening to very different podcasts, but on average I absorb seven to ten shows per week.

A decade ago, when podcasts were in their infancy, most shows were amateurish and clunky. Though that turned off some listeners, today podcasts have matured and quality is, in many cases, superb. In fact, The Washington Post featured a story in the fall of 2014 proclaiming podcasts to not only be back and bigger than ever, but now also profitable. Podcasts are so easy to produce and distribute, and so many people (consumers with disposable income) are seeking this form of knowledge/entertainment that this creates an opportunity. Could this be an opportunity for you? I believe it could, but remember: Your goal is not to simply hear yourself talk. Your goal is to unashamedly monetize the podcast by informing, inspiring and/or entertaining, so you can fund your lifestyle by fulfilling the listener's needs.

For a great example of a homesteader doing this, look no further than Jack Spirko. Jack recorded the first episode of The Survival Podcast in 2008 during his daily 50-mile commute between his office and home in Arlington, Texas. The audio quality was marginal and the background noise pronounced, but it did not matter. What did matter was Jack's enthusiasm to share his passion for survivalism, preparedness, and homesteading. That passion is critically important to a successful podcast, because so many shows start and then burn out quickly. Jack's passion enabled him to record a DAILY podcast, and just as he was sharing his thoughts and knowledge during his commute, a large number of consumers began listening to him during theirs. The result? Fast forward now to 2014 where Jack has recorded nearly 1,500 episodes and up to 100,000 people per day download The Survival Podcast. He has also smartly monetized his show with podcast advertising, blog advertising, a membership site on The Survival Podcast website and other ways that expand beyond The Survival Podcast show itself.

Before you attempt to emulate Jack's success, let me offer a word of caution about podcasting. Earlier, I mentioned that Amazon makes it easy for new authors to create books, but at the same time, that places a much larger burden on the author to ensure cover design, formatting, editing, and proofreading, content and so on are professionally handled. Far too many authors fail in this regard, and the same can be said for podcasting. It is technically easy to plug a microphone into your computer, record a podcast in Garageband, and upload it to a hosting and distribution service. This in itself does not make a good podcast. Beyond the obvious need for an excellent microphone and consistent audio quality, it takes enthusiasm, tight delivery, excellent content, CONSISTENCY and, if you conduct interviews, excellent and engaging hosts who are aligned with the show's mission. This can be achieved, as Jack demonstrates, as long as you approach it as seriously as he did.

There you have it, just a sampling of ways you can use your skills to get money from the farm fairy, often very good money, while living your dream life off the land. For modern homesteaders, the Internet creates a global market and, unlike with physical products, it does not matter where you are geographically located if you are offering virtual/online/writing services.

Chapter Four
Make Money Selling Farmstead Products

"It is the sweet, simple things of life which are the real ones after all."

— Laura Ingalls Wilder

The last two chapters presented numerous ways to use either skills or land as a platform from which to generate income on the homestead. In some cases, the income potential is very significant, rivaling that of a decent-size entrepreneurial endeavor while in other cases, the income potential is quite modest and less demanding. Here, I will share some of the most common ways of producing and selling products from the homestead.

Some of these product ideas are only possible because you have land; for example, marketing your own meat products. Others cross over into services, such as farmstead photography. I suspect you have already noticed many of these areas overlap, as in the case that often land is needed to create a sizable skills-based business. You will get the idea, and in chapter six I will show you how to put the puzzle together and Personalize Your Homestead Plan. For now, let us focus on tangible products.

FARMSTEAD MEATS

Organic, grass-fed, sustainably raised, free-range, pastured, heritage… these descriptive phrases are becoming more commonly recognized, because there is a constantly expanding market of consumers looking to connect with and support farmers who are tending the earth ethically. These consumers are just as anxious to support the local community as they are to tell Monsanto and confined animal feeding operations (CAFOs) where to shove it.

When you sell meats directly from the farm, you have numerous decisions to make. The first choice may be if you want to sell bulk (whole/half/quarter) animals or small retail packages. If you sell bulk, then you can avoid the hassles of becoming licensed to store packaged meats in your farm freezers by technically selling a "live" animal to the consumer. You then deliver the animal to the processor and the consumer determines how they want the animal butchered, pays the processor directly, and picks up their cuts. The consumer saves money on a per pound basis and you save headaches.

Alternatively, you can sell individual packaged cuts such as roasts, ground beef, pork chops, chicken breasts, rack of lamb and so on to consumers. In the case of red meats (beef, lamb and pork), this requires you to have meats processed by a state- or USDA-inspected facility. You must also follow regulations for storing and transporting your labeled products, which often requires multiple licenses. Do not let that stop you, as the regulations are not that

Grass-fed beef package

burdensome in most places. However, the costs for freezers, utilities, and transportation must be considered. The bottom line is that it is much easier on you to sell bulk cuts (whole/half/quarter animal) and let the customer pick the meat up at the processor, but you will reach a much larger market by selling individually packaged retail cuts. After all, there are more people able to buy a pack of ground beef than there are who can store half a cow!

Other options for selling meats are wholesale, retail, and restaurants. The above options that sell directly to customers constitute direct marketing. You will get the highest price selling that way, but you will also expend the most effort and need the most marketing savvy for sure. Selling to wholesalers or distributors could put your products on retail shelves, but it takes time and effort to set up these relationships. If you do succeed in setting up these relationships, it will later be easier to add your other farm products (below) to those distribution channels.

Many farmsteaders want to sell to restaurants, and for good reason. If you are near the right markets, there are many fine chefs who value delicious and local ingredients, and you want to sell to people who value what you produce. Some chefs want smaller portions and packaged cuts that you are selling directly to customers. If that is the case, you probably will not have much room to discount prices unless the chefs commit to larger bulk quantities or weekly deliveries, since your costs will not be any lower. In larger markets, however, chefs at leading restaurants will want whole animals (or many animals) so they can break down (butcher) the animal themselves. This has the same benefit to you of selling whole animals to individual consumers while also giving your farm brand the cachet of being prominently featured on a fine restaurant's menu.

There is much more to say on this topic, but the point is to give you ideas and get you thinking about what works for you. For many farmsteaders, selling farm-raised meats will be the heart of their income-generating engine.

Variations - In many states you may be able to process poultry (which includes rabbit) on your farm and not use an inspected processor by following a Public Law 90-492 Exemption. Read carefully and check with your state regulators before proceeding.

FARM FRESH MILK

Admit it... the phrase conjures images of the old milk truck, glass bottles on the doorstep and old-fashioned wholesomeness. Consumers today have become so disconnected from the sources of their food that many do not even realize they are drinking an ultra-pasteurized product that was "formerly" milk until they read an article about it or hear it mentioned on the news. When their eyes are opened, many go looking for real milk, usually raw, from a local farmer. And they are willing to pay anywhere from $5 to $15 per gallon for it depending on where they are in the country, and whether the cow was fed grain and silage (least expensive milk) or was purely grass-fed (most expensive milk). Be sure to operate within the implicit and explicit laws of your state. Also check out the Weston A. Price campaign for real milk, and if you decide to sell milk, list yourself there.

Variations - butter, buttermilk, yogurt, etc. if you are able to pasteurize the milk first

FARMSTEAD CHEESE

As I said in chapter one, if you are milking cows, sheep or goats anyway, why not turn the milk into delicious farmstead cheese? Farmstead cheese is cheese that you produce from the milk of YOUR animals, whereas artisanal cheese is cheese you produce with milk you buy from another dairy. Either way, you will need a state-approved and inspected cheese operation and anywhere from a modest investment (several thousand dollars) to a major investment (several hundred thousand dollars) to purchase land, fencing, animals, a milking parlor, and set up a cheese-production room, ripening room, cheese cave, purchase cheese-production equipment (vats, presses, molds, etc.) and so on. There is no denying that it takes a major investment to become a farmstead cheesemaker, but for many, the lifestyle and payoff is undeniably alluring. I very much enjoy my relationship to my cows and the art of making cheese.

In comparison to purely artisanal cheese, <u>farmstead may offer the following ADVANTAGES</u>:

- Greater control over milk quality
- Greater control over milk costs, and therefore greater control over your business
- Marketing advantage and real competitive uniqueness of your own terroir
- Greater profit-margin potential
- Ancillary income from young cows/goats/sheep as you breed for milk production
- Potential for other business spin offs (sell fluid milk, ice cream/butter, tours, etc.)
- You know the milk quality and any changes that could affect cheese makes (feed changes, pasture, hay, etc.)

However, <u>farmstead may offer the following DISADVANTAGES</u> in comparison to artisanal:

- Tied to milking daily, including holidays, birthdays and rainy days
- Much higher start-up costs (land, livestock, buildings, water, septic, equipment, etc.)
- Tied to making cheese daily or multiple times per week
- Lost production when animals are ill or mastitis strikes
- Ongoing vet costs, since you own the animals
- Need to breed the animals and ensure a tight breeding window
- Ongoing/rising feed costs, including labor/equipment to handle feed

- Dual managerial requirements (animal husbandry and cheesemaking)
- Maintenance costs of milking system, cleaning chemicals, etc.
- Licensing and inspection requirements

Chapter two describes farmstead cheese in detail, since it requires a sizable acreage to offer this product. But since it is a product, I briefly mention it in this chapter also, because I want to share with you a profile of a wonderful couple who enjoy a beautiful, self-sufficient lifestyle.

PROFILE # 11

"Becoming more self-sufficient does not require leaving a "real job." It is a state of mind and approach to life that can be done anywhere, on any level."

– Karen Mickler and Bruce DeGroot

Photo: samenglish.com

Who: Yellow Branch Cheese, Bruce DeGroot and Karen Mickler (YellowBranch.com)

Where: Graham County, NC

Homestead/Farm Highlights: 60-plus acres of mountain land, including 10 acres of pasture; 2 barns with attached cheese-making facility; 2 homes (one personal dwelling and one rental). We rent 5 acres of pasture. Adjacent to the farm property, Karen has a pottery studio with retail gallery for selling pots and cheese.

What were your "real jobs" prior to breaking away to become more self-sufficient? We did not break away from real jobs to become more self-sufficient. Our way of life in North Carolina is an extension of the life we were living in Iowa, growing and preserving our own food as well as making butter and yogurt. We purchased the farm with Bruce's family in 1981 and continued our work of carpentry, woodworking, pottery, and a self-sufficient way of life.

What inspired you into wanting to be more self-sufficient? Karen: After college, I discovered I was drawn to gardening and growing my own food. It is fun and rewarding to grow, harvest, and preserve delicious and nutritious food. Some of my most satisfying moments are in the garden. **Bruce**: In high school, I became interested in self-sufficiency in food and work, and set about acquiring the skills: carpentry, construction, gardening and moving to rural environments.

What was the most challenging thing about taking the leap to your new life? If we had known we would end up establishing a dairy, we would have acquired a more suitable farm. We are challenged by the lack of pasture and the subsequent limitation on the number of cows we can support to produce milk for the cheese.

What are your sources of income now? Cheesemaking and pottery.

What inspired you to become a cheesemaker and why did you choose farmstead cheesemaking instead of artisanal cheesemaking? We purchased a milk cow with another family the first year we moved here. Their children did not care for the milk, so we inherited the cow and three gallons of milk a day. Learning to make cheese naturally followed. We were producing more cheese than we could eat, and studied the feasibility of becoming a licensed facility and did so. There are no other dairies in the area, and we were not interested in purchasing milk for our cheeses.

How did you learn to make cheese? Initially, from the many books we had on hand and experimentation, and from visits to other cheesemakers. One of our first mentors was Angelo LaPaglia who owned Erie Cheese Making Supply Co. Membership in the American Cheese Society also provided workshops and contacts with other professionals. Karen also attended short courses in cheesemaking in Canada and Wisconsin.

How did you get into the pottery business and how does running that business compare to the cheese business? What are the pros and cons? Karen took a pottery class after college and eventually had a two-year apprenticeship at an Iowa pottery while working part time. After a stint as an over-the-road truck driver, she had the confidence to open her own pottery studio, selling her wares at art fairs and retail stores.

Bruce learned carpentry and woodworking during his college years and gained work experience in both. Running any business requires knowledge of product development, quality control, marketing, bookkeeping, and continuing education. Having prior business experience was very helpful in running the cheese business.

Cheesemaking requires meeting regulatory standards and working with the agencies that oversee the standards. Bruce's carpentry skills were instrumental in building the infrastructure for the farm, pottery, dwellings, and cheesemaking business. The pottery and cheese business are separate legal entities, but marketed as a unit. The pros: We find we have a lot more visitors to our retail shop because of the combined marketing. Some come for cheese, some for pottery; some are drawn to the combination.

Starting a business for the first time can be scary. How did you figure out the rules and regulatory issues for starting your farm? Do you have a marketing background? We contacted the local NC Extension agency and they guided us to the regulatory agencies. We also did our own research and acquired a working knowledge of the regulations. Everyone we contacted was very helpful and encouraging. We partnered with agricultural and craft organizations, as well as tourism groups and chambers of commerce.

What advice do you have for someone considering leaving a "real job" to become more self-sufficient? Becoming more self-sufficient does not require leaving a "real job." It is a state of mind and approach to life that can be done anywhere, on any level. Being self-sufficient is not a simple life and requires a lot of dedication and perseverance.

ARTISANAL CHEESE

By contrast to farmstead cheese production, artisan cheese production does not require that you own the milking animals. Rather, you are free to purchase milk from other approved sources. This offers numerous financial and scheduling benefits. For example, consider the following pros and cons.

Artisanal may offer the following ADVANTAGES over farmstead:

- Greater lifestyle flexibility, since you do not have to milk every day, and can choose when you want to make cheese
- Much lower start-up costs, since you do not have to invest in land, livestock and milking equipment
- A much more mobile business, should you choose to relocate
- No need to deal with breeding/calving (lambing, etc.)
- Can focus solely on cheese
- Can scale up more easily
- Can buy and use milk from multi-species

Artisanal may offer the following DISADVANTAGES compared to farmstead:

- Milk costs may go up unannounced, and you likely cannot make it up
- Your milk provider could raise prices, cease selling and sell raw milk directly, or sell to someone else (How would that impact your business?)

- No uniqueness to your terroir
- How will you deliver/transport that much milk?
- You may not know about changes in milk (feed, etc.) that could effect cheese make

For many cheesemakers, artisanal proved to be a more enticing option. In some cases, they were already locked into a small homestead that offered enough room to create a cheese-production environment but not enough for a milking parlor and grazing land. In other cases, cheesemakers were literally located in high-density suburban neighborhoods and wanted to make cheese there to access the high-volume traffic. In that case, they purchased milk from the countryside (creating a value-added income stream for that farmer ;-) and used it to make cheese in the city.

Let us take a look at a profile of another excellent cheesemaker who opted for the artisan cheese route instead of farmstead cheese.

PROFILE # 12

> "I like working at a job that yields something concrete and real at the end of the day."
>
> – Jennifer Perkins

Who: Jennifer Perkins, Cheesemaker and Owner of Looking Glass Creamery (AshevilleCheese.com)

Where: Fairview, NC in Western North Carolina About 10 miles outside of Asheville, NC

Homestead/Farm Highlights: We have less than two acres in an increasingly suburban setting in what was historically a farming community but has succumbed to development.

What was your "real job" prior to breaking away to become more self-sufficient? I spent 10 years working towards the goal of starting a cheesemaking operation with employment in the dairy industry, internships, and classes. I also worked at two destination properties (The Biltmore Estate and Blackberry Farm), which really helped me recognize the importance of branding, telling a story, and creating experiences for people. My "real" jobs prior to that were mostly in accounting and operations management. That background made managing the books and the administrative side of the business a lot easier.

What inspired (or scared) you into wanting to be more self-sufficient? I was motivated by the prospect of starting a successful business that contributed to the local community, supported small independent dairy farming, and connected people more directly to their food and educated them about the craft of cheesemaking.

When (if) you left your "real job" in suburbia, what was the most challenging thing about taking the leap to your new life? The most challenging hurdle was not so much starting the business but being unable to run it by myself when it had grown, two years into its operation. We decided that Andy, my husband, would also have to quit his job in corporate America and leave his career path to work full time in the business to continue its growth. It was then that the safety net of a regular paycheck and health insurance for our family fell away and the reality of the risk we were taking became much more real.

What are your sources of income? Income? What Income? We do not have any income from any other place other than the business. We live off repaying ourselves on our initial investment into the business. We are in year six and we still do not generate a profit, but we are able to pay our bills and employees and taxes, and have continually reinvested in the business with upgraded equipment, better packaging, etc., so hopefully profit will follow soon.

What inspired you to become a cheesemaker? A connection with animals is part of what brought me to the craft. I enjoy working with livestock, managing herds, and the proximity to the cycle of life and connection to the weather and world around you that farming provides. I really became fascinated with cheesemaking as a craft and loved the historical context of "preserving" the harvest of spring and summer for the dark, cold months of winter. I also like working at a job that yields something concrete and real at the end of the day. And finally, the amazing variety of cheeses and influence you can have over the process and how varied the final result can be from very similar beginnings.

Why did you choose artisanal cheesemaking instead of farmstead cheesemaking? Out of necessity mostly, but now that we have, I am very glad we choose this path. We live about 20 minutes outside of a very food-centric and tourist-driven town. To afford the amount of land we would need to start a farmstead operation, we would have had to move 30 or more miles farther outside town and in the mountains an hour drive or more away. Our proximity to our customer base made everything from agritourism to delivery times much easier. With our limited financial resources, no family locally to help, or children old enough to assist with the business managing the two distinct demands of dairying and cheesemaking would have overwhelmed us. We have been able to build partnerships with two local dairy farmers who provide us with great milk for cheesemaking. Prior to us starting our business, there was no market in this area for small dairy farms to sell their milk legally. Our business has helped other farm businesses grow and other cheesemakers have followed in our footsteps.

How did you learn to make cheese? Lots of trial and error at home. Classes at NC State and with Peter Dixon of Dairy Foods Consulting. Unpaid apprenticeship at a farmstead goat dairy in Southern VA and employment as Assistant Cheesemaker / Dairy Technician in the sheep operation at Blackberry Farm.

If you left a "real job" in suburbia, what was the most challenging thing about taking the leap to your new life? No paycheck, no health insurance.

Starting a business for the first time can be scary. How did you market your classes and cheese to get customers? Do you have

a marketing background? I do not have a marketing background but find that I am pretty good at it. Starting a business has helped me find skills I never knew I had. We started small, learned, and grew slowly. We advertise through word of mouth, social media, good packaging, a good website, winning recognition or awards, sending out press releases, networking and staying in touch with key people.

If starting over, what would you do differently? Have more money in the bank in the beginning to help with cash flow and bulk buying. Some additional infrastructure like a second aging room, included a drying room, had HVAC system instead of space heaters and window AC. Incorporated a loading dock into our building and having better parking for customers. Most importantly, I would have built the agritourism component into the business from the start instead of adding it in at year 5. Having an on-site store has been very beneficial over the past year and helped us adjust our ratio of wholesale to retail customers to a better balance.

What do you miss about city/urban life...you know, the "real" world? We still have our feet in both worlds given our business model but we live pretty close to the bone financially. Being able to take a real vacation every once in a while would be nice and less concern about money in leaner months would be an improvement.

What advice do you have for someone considering leaving a "real job" to become more self-sufficient? Get good financial advice before you take the leap. I still feel there are things I do not know about managing our business in the most financially beneficial way.

Have a passion for what you do and a vision for where you want your business to go, because it is harder to build the business you want if you do not know what that means for you.

Starting a small business means you have to get comfortable selling yourself as much as your product.

Be flexible. You have to be willing to find a way around, under or over obstacles; sometimes that means charging forward with dogged determination and other times it means changing your plan.

Expect everything to cost twice as much and take twice as long as you think it will.

FARM FRESH EGGS

If you raise your hens on pasture, then you will be producing the most beautiful and nutritious eggs available anywhere. Just check out the chart below from Mother Earth News and take a moment to read their fine article on the benefit of free-range eggs. This research emphasizes chicken eggs, but keep in mind that not all egg varieties are the same. Many consumers will pay much more for duck eggs than chicken eggs, and you can also sell hatching eggs (turkey, geese, ducks, chicken, guinea, etc.) instead of eating eggs. The point is that your egg-laying feathered friends can do more than beautify your landscape; they can generate profits, too.

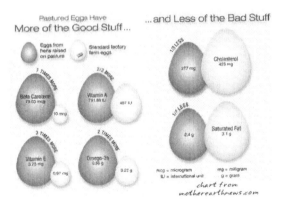

VEGETABLES AND HERBS

There is not much limit to what you can grow for consumers and restaurants. Warm and cool-season vegetables, fresh flowers, herbs, you name it. You will have the same choices to make regarding selling (direct, restaurants, retail, wholesale) as you do with meats, but there is one big difference. Whereas meats can be stored frozen for months, the value in vegetables is to be sold fresh, often the day they are harvested. So it is critical to establish strong customer relationships first either by having a solid relationship with restaurants or by operating a CSA for individual customers.

FRUITS

Strawberries, blueberries, blackberries, cranberries, peaches, apples, figs, melons… get the idea? Almost everyone has a sweet tooth and these fruits can be harvested, sold, and delivered directly to farmers markets, restaurants or consumers, or you can offer pick-your-own options. And, in comparison to vegetables and even small-scale livestock, fruit production tends to require less labor and promises some time off. For example, our strawberry beds produce like crazy for two months of the year and require daily harvesting, washing, etc., but for the rest of the year, not too much work is involved. By contrast, chickens require daily feeding, checking water, and watching out for predators.

Fruits, like some vegetables, also provide the opportunity to create and market value-added products, such as jams, jellies, chutneys and the like. These have the benefit of being shelf-stable, unlike fresh fruit, and could even be made using your own sweeteners if you raise honey bees!

SWEETENERS

Maple syrup, honey, and sorghum syrup all come to mind. With concerns about allergies increasing, I expect a continued rise in the demand for local honey. All you need is to make or buy some bee boxes, get a bag of bees and a queen or a nuc and let them pollinate your garden. Then you are on your way to the sweet life!

We raise several hives of honeybees and have been doing so since we began our homesteading adventure. If you think you may be interested in this, check out *The Backyard Beekeeper* by Kim Flottum or *The Complete Step-by-Step Book of Beekeeping* by David Cramp.

FARM CRAFTS

You will likely find countless supplies on your farmstead that can be marketed and sold to crafters, such as rabbit pelts, turkey and peacock feathers, wood cuttings, wool and more. Could you take raw lumber and produce elegant cutting boards or cheese trays? Take a look on Etsy or eBay to see what is selling and then see what you have. For inspiration, look no further than Patrice Lewis. She and her husband not only created a wonderful woodcraft business that has sustained them for two decades, but Patrice is an excellent author of both the rural-revolution.com website and several books. She frequently shares her homesteading wisdom with readers of Backwoods Home Magazine, Country Living Magazine and other publications. Be sure to read her book *The Simplicity Primer* after finishing this one.

PROFILE # 13

"The right mindset can go a long way toward getting you through hard times."

— Patrice Lewis

Who: Patrice Lewis, Rural-Revolution.com

Where: Rural north Idaho

What: Twenty-acre homestead (mostly prairie, some trees) where we raise cattle for beef and milk, chickens for eggs and meat, a large garden, fruit trees (start up), small fruits, and occasionally a half-acre wheat patch

Were you always a homesteader, or did you leave a "real job" prior to breaking away to become more self-sufficient? Both my husband and I grew up in small towns but had no real rural upbringings. When we got married, we commuted along crowded highways to conventional 9-to-5 jobs for two years. Then came the morning of the "commute from hell" with a bad accident that tied us up in traffic for two hours (in the days before cell phones). When we got home at the end of the day, we looked at each other and said, "We have to get out of here."

We had no real notion of a farm at that point, but we knew we wanted to live rural. Within a year, we had moved to southwest

Oregon and bought a fixer-upper on four acres. I was in grad school full time, and since my husband could not find work in his field, he started our woodcraft business.

What inspired (or scared) you into wanting to be more self-sufficient? A long time ago I heard an eerie sentiment: That most Americans would starve standing next to a cow in a field of ripe wheat. Meaning: Most Americans are too ignorant to feed themselves from elemental food sources. I must have read that forty years ago, and I never forgot it. It started an itch to learn as much as possible about food independence. When Don and I got married, that notion was vaguely in the backs of our minds, but did not come into focus until we moved to Oregon and we had a bit of elbow room to experiment with small-scale homesteading.

If you left a "real job" in suburbia, what was the most challenging thing about taking the leap to your new life? A lack of financial security. We were DINKS (Double Income, No Kids) when we moved, and we went from a generous combined income to an income of ZERO. We were without income for five months while my husband finalized his design for our woodcrafts, before we had our first show. We survived on credit cards, student loans (I was in grad school full time), and our small savings account.

We had to learn frugality to the nth degree, and learn it fast. It was hard at the time but probably one of the best lessons we ever received. That frugality has never left us and has served us well in a bad economy.

What are your income streams? How do you generate income, including off-farm, if relevant? We have four income streams: our woodcraft business (still our primary source of support); an online business (details are confidential); my writing; and occasional income from the farm, i.e. selling heifers.

If starting over, what would you do differently? We would probably not just up and quit our day jobs, but instead seek out employment to ease the transition. If we knew then that we would be embarking on a decade of poverty, I do not know if we would have had the courage to do it. Yet it all turned out well in the end, and taught us many valuable lessons.

What do you miss about city/urban life... you know, the "real" world?

Hmmmmm.

Nothing.

What advice do you have for someone considering leaving a "real job" to become more self-sufficient? Get out of debt. Learn to be REALLY frugal now, before you move. Develop income streams NOW, before you leap. Look for any and all ways to work from home (most rural people wear multiple hats and have multiple "irons in the fire" for income). Do not bite off more than you can chew (financially) when it comes to your country home – in other words, don't buy a McMansion. Your income is likely to drop precipitously once you move, and you do not want to be overburdened with too much debt in your new home. Unless you have a lot of spare cash, do not buy bare land – it is far more expensive than you think once you start drilling wells, bring in power (either conventional or off-grid), building a house and/or outbuildings, fencing, etc.

Make sure all family members are on board before moving rural. A sullen spouse or teenage kids will not make for a pleasant transition.

And oddly, develop the attitude that you WILL make it in the country, that failure is not an option. The right mindset can go a long way toward getting you through hard times.

Appreciate your spouse and all he or she does. Spousal support is critical, and you will be "socializing" with your spouse far more than before. Hopefully this will bring you closer, not tear you apart.

Develop a sense of humor. You will need it, and it will carry you through hard times.

Pray. Never hurts, often helps.

JEWELRY

Rather than selling craft supplies from the farm, why not make your own jewelry! Think of using feathers from peacocks, turkeys, guineas, or geese. Or, perhaps you have a large deer population and you will find lots of shed antlers in late winter. These and more can be used to make unique (aka one-of-a-kind) pieces of jewelry.

Looking for a little inspiration? Check out etsy.com and look through hundreds of examples of handmade jewelry items produced by home-based crafters. And if you do not want to produced finished products, you can also sell raw materials from your farm on Etsy to help others create their craft. What kind of materials? How about heritage turkey feathers, unique dried flowers or herbs, wool and even farm "things" you no longer use, such as waterers, feeders, etc.

Variation - Instead of jewelry, make rustic woodworking gifts from your downed trees. Think of tables, willow furniture, log furniture, kitchen utensils… whatever you can dream up..

WINE AND BEER

Due to stringent regulations you may not want to produce wine and beer, but what about becoming an accomplice? Could you grow local hops for the beer market or grapes for local wineries using your land? I bet you could and that few people are!

VALUE-ADDED PRODUCTS

I will not attempt to list all the ways you can add value to products that you could produce on the farm, and many require some regulatory approval. But if you are up for it, imagine:

- Farm-fresh baby food,
- Dog treats,
- Lard,
- Jams,
- Salsa,
- Grains,
- Pickles,
- Sauerkraut… the list goes on.

Do not be afraid to seek regulatory approval as it is not as difficult as you might think. Just call the health department or your state department of agriculture and find out what you need to do to comply. Others do it and so can you.

PRODUCE AND SELL HONEY

It is relatively easy to produce and sell honey, and profitable as well. Once you are established, your bees will do a good job of reproduction and, since they require no feed, the cost of producing honey is virtually nil once you have made the initial investment in bees, boxes, clothing, and equipment. And there is always a good market for honey, especially local honey with the increasing prevalence of allergies. Still, do not expect to make a lot of money selling honey, unless you expect to have A LOT of hives. Barriers to entry are low, meaning competitors can pop up quickly, but beekeeping is an excellent sideline business that not only can serve as a "gateway" product to drive customers to your homestead but has the added benefit of pollinating your crops.

If you are interested in bees but new to the hobby, check out the forums at beesource.com.

GROW AND SELL UNIQUE FEED

A few years ago I watched Mike Rowe of Discovery Channel's popular television show Dirty Jobs do a feature on a business located about an hour south of me. In the show, Rowe visited Ghann's Crickets, which breeds and sells crickets, worms and feeder insect supplies to a national market. According to their website, the business began when Aubrey Ghann quit his job as a welder in 1952 to begin raising crickets. Of course folks thought he was crazy, just as some may question your motives, but today Ghann's represents a business model that you could learn from. Could you grow high-protein food for chickens that is more natural than conventional feed? Perhaps...

PRODUCE AND SELL GARDEN TRANSPLANTS

If you love the idea of growing and gardening, here is an idea. Become proficient at seed starting and selling garden transplants. To differentiate yourself, why not specialize only in heirloom varieties and offer packages of plants that are companions? You could also offer growing guides to show customers how to nurture their plants to fruition, thereby further differentiating yourself.

MUSHROOMS

Cultivate mushrooms for consumers or restaurants and, if you live among chanterelles, morels, etc., learn to hunt and sell these delicacies at farmers markets and to restaurants! This is both a skill that you will appreciate as a prepper/survivalist as well as one that can generate seasonal income for you.

PHOTOGRAPHY

I mentioned photography in the last chapter as a skill and it certainly is that, but your rare-breed animals and quaint rural landscape offer you unique resources to create poetic imagery. You could add value by printing and creating frames from your woodlot and selling through various resorts and stores in your state, or license use of your high-resolution images through the various providers listed in the last chapter.

MAKE CUSTOM TOOLS FOR HOMESTEADERS

Necessity is the mother of all invention, they say, and farmers are an inventive group. If you know how or want to learn to make knives from rustic materials such as spent saw blades, antlers, wood, etc., you may find a ready market. Or, perhaps you will find the need to develop tools to tend your garden such as two of our favorite garden tools, the Wheel Hoe and the Hooke 'n Crooke.

Or you could offer plans on how to build them yourself like the folks at WhizBang did. Read Herrick's story, below, of how he kept his "day job" in the city while homesteading in the country and combined both experiences to develop and market products for homesteaders.

PROFILE # 14

"I could spend the rest of my life on my land here in the boondocks, never go to a city again, and be perfectly content."

– Herrick Kimball

Who: Herrick Kimball, whizbangbooks.blogspot.com

Where: Finger Lakes region of upstate New York.

What was/is your "real job" prior to becoming more self-sufficient? I worked for 23 years as a carpenter and home remodeler. Then I worked 13 years in the NY State prisons system. I left the state job in 2013 (at 55 years old) to work at my "Planet Whizbang" home business full time. To have a profitable, home-based mail order business is something I have wanted since I was 16 years old (it only took me 39 years).

What inspired/scared you to start down the road to becoming more self-sufficient? The idea of living a simple, debt-free, self-reliant lifestyle resonated with me when I was a teenager in the early 1970s. I was inspired by books like Helen and Scott Nearing's *Living The Good Life*, and Gene Logsdon's *Two Acre Eden*.

Homestead/Farm Highlights: When my wife and I married in 1980, we lived in a small apartment in town. Our goal was to save enough money to buy a small piece of land and build our own home, and that is what we did. We bought 1.5 acres of rural land, most of it woods and gully. The useable area for a home and garden is not much bigger than a large lot in the suburbs.

We built a small (16' x 24') home in 1982 and have added on to the house a couple times since. We have never had a bank loan.

In 2012, our longtime desire to have more land came true when we purchased 16 acres of woods, field, and a stream right next to our 1.5 acre homestead. We were able to purchase the land, debt free (the only way we would ever have done it) with saved profits from the Planet Whizbang mail-order business. The land came with a house, where our son and his family now live.

What are your income streams? My wife left work to be a full-time mother when our first child was born in 1988 and we have lived on my income alone since then. I never made much money as a carpenter and we went through some real lean times trying to make ends meet. Only in the last few years have we had an excess of income, and that has all come through the success of the Planet Whizbang home business.

As for income streams, one of my objectives with Planet Whizbang is to develop multiple streams of income from multiple products that I sell. The business started in 2011 with a self-published book about how to make a chicken plucker. Then I started selling some of the parts needed to make a chicken plucker. I developed plans and products for a Whizbang cider-making system, and for Whizbang gardening. Most recently I have started making Classic American Clothespins.

The how-to books I have self-published generate an income stream, but the poultry plucker parts I sell generate the most income.

Why did you choose rural homesteading versus urban homesteading? I grew up in a suburban housing project outside Syracuse. New York. When I was in 9th grade, my family moved to an old farm house on 25 acres out in the country. That move was a life-changing experience. So I have experienced urban/suburban life and I want nothing to do with it. More importantly, I did not want my children (three boys) to grow up in a suburban culture. My wife is a farmer's daughter, so she naturally loves country life.

Why did you choose writing guides and books for income generation, and how did you learn to make a chicken plucker? Writing how-to information is a natural talent and impulse for me. I discovered the talent back in 1992 when I sent the start of an article idea to Fine Homebuilding magazine. That was the beginning of my part-time career as a professional writer. I wrote numerous articles for Fine Homebuilding over the next few years, then I wrote three how-to books for The Taunton Press.

In 1998 my family started raising chickens for meat (we raised them only for eggs previously). Plucking the fatted fowl on butchering day was a real chore. I found out that there were mechanical pluckers that made the job a whole lot easier, but they were expensive. So I went looking for plans for a homemade plucking machine. There were no good plans out there. I saw that as a creative opportunity. With 24 years of carpentry experience and on-the-job problem-solving skills, it was a relatively easy project. I patterned my simple, wood-frame plucker after the expensive stainless steel pluckers.

I made, modified and tested a few plucker prototypes before I had a plan that I was happy with. It would pluck two chickens clean in 15 seconds! Just flip the switch, drop the birds in, and the machine does all the work. My plucker can be built by anyone with basic handyman tools and skills for less money than a brand new plucking machine.

The word "whizbang" came to my mind when I saw my homemade plucker at work. I looked up the word in a dictionary and found it means, "conspicuous for speed, excellence or startling effect." It is the perfect name.

Starting a business for the first-time can be scary. How did you market your books? Starting a business is not scary for me. It is exciting! From a young age I have been an idea person, with an entrepreneurial urge. My first serious self-employment venture was a chimney cleaning business I started when I was 19. I was also self-employed as a remodeling contractor for many years.

I started self-publishing books and building my Planet Whizbang mail order business as a part-time enterprise while I worked at the prison job full time. I worked hard at developing and promoting new products, hoping (and praying) that the business might prosper enough that I could break free from the full-time, wage-slave job. And that is what eventually happened.

As for marketing books (and the numerous other products I sell through Planet Whizbang), the success I have realized would not have come without the Internet. My blog (thedeliberateagrarian. com), the various blog-format web sites I have created, Yahoo discussion groups, and YouTube movies are all free and they are powerful marketing tools.

If starting over again on the path to self-sufficiency, what would you do differently? In retrospect, there is not much I would do differently. My objective from a young age was to acquire useful skills, NOT acquire debt, build my own home in the country, get married, raise a family, and live a simplified lifestyle that is not totally dependent on the industrial system.

The only thing I might do differently is buy more than 1.5 acres of land. It seemed like enough when we bought it, but 5 to 10 acres would have been better for all the homestead and home business projects we have had.

I should also point out that if the Internet was around when I was a teenager, you can bet I would have been using it to market and sell products.

What do you miss about city/urban life...you know, the "real" world? I do not consider city and urban life to be the real world. It is an artificial world, sustained by the agrarian world around it. I could spend the rest of my life on my land here in the boondocks of rural New York state, never go to a city again, and be perfectly content.

What advice do you have for someone considering leaving a "real job" to become more self-sufficient? A person or family can become more self-sufficient while working a wage-slave job to pay the necessary bills. While working the wage-slave job, you can seriously pursue the elimination of all debt. Simplify your wants and needs in every way possible, while acquiring tools and skills of self-reliance.

Beyond that, develop an entrepreneurial mindset and look for small business opportunities. It is almost impossible to pay the industrial-world bills with a small farm these days. But it is entirely possible to create a home business that pays the bills and allows a family to live a down-to-earth, more self-reliant lifestyle on a section of productive land.

Being home, on my land, with my family around me, not dependent on a job to pay the bills, and living a contra-industrial lifestyle is my definition of success and freedom.

BUILDING CHICKEN/RABBIT TRACTORS

When urban folks see your fancy chicken coops and tractors they will likely want one of their own. They will not have the time or skill to make it, but they will have the money to buy it. Market directly to them through local organics associations, conferences, publications, and online groups.

One of the author's rabbit pens

MANURE & COMPOST

Okay, put your marketing hat on now… you are not selling a load of horse s*#t, you are selling organic fertility! Better yet, nutrients! From worm castings to rabbit pellets and, yes, horse manure, you are selling what everyone needs for healthy plants and topsoil.

ARTISAN MEAT PRODUCTS

You do not see many people doing this because, as with cheesemaking, there is skill, investment, and regulatory compliance required. And therein lies the opportunity! Imagine making pancetta, pepperoni, saucisson sec, salami or Iberico style long-aged cured ham from your rare-breed pigs that consumed acorns and whey. Know anyone else in your state doing this? In your entire region? Is that sausage I smell or is it opportunity?

PROFILE # 15

> "We were always drawn to a simpler lifestyle, enjoying nature and the outdoors."
>
> – Doug Hill

Who: Doug and Lori Hill, CabinCreekHeritageFarm.com

Where: Upper Marlboro, MD (Prince Georges County)

If you had a "real job" prior to breaking away to pursue a more self-sufficient lifestyle, what was it that you left? Doug had a successful career in IT. Through his career, he has evolved from heads-down engineering to more and more of business focus. While Doug is still in IT today as a partner in an IT firm, he started the family farm using this business focus. Over the coming years, God willing, we hope to work completely within the family business.

What inspired (or scared) you into pursuing a more self-sufficient lifestyle? We were always drawn to a simpler lifestyle, enjoying nature and the outdoors. Wherever we have lived, we spent a majority of our time outdoors, working on the yard, heading out to camp somewhere, or simply playing with the kids in the backyard. As our children reached school age, we found the community we lived in was far different from the communities we grew up in largely due to the two-income families. No one was ever home. Living in the suburbs, along with all of its challenges, we opted to move to the country, seeking a wholesome environment to raise our family.

We were not in the country very long before a few sheep appeared one Christmas causing our husbandry skills to begin developing. Shortly after this, a box of chicks brought delicious proteins and hen management. Years later, we learned that pigs love the woodlands (most of our farm). With a decade of learning on the farm, we kicked off a commercial venture focused at local, sustainable farming.

Homestead/Farm Highlights: Our family farm is a one-generation, two-year-old farm of about 25 acres. Mostly woodlands, on the outskirts of the Washington DC suburbs. Our focus is on raising livestock using sustainable heritage practices. Our primary focus is woodland-raised, Berkshire pork, pastured chickens, and soy-free, pastured eggs. Seasonally, we offer grass-fed/finished lamb. Recently, we have begun offering value-added products including Charcuterie and Goat-Milk Soap.

What are your income streams? Whole/Half animals, CSA, on-farm store, farmers markets, wholesale to local businesses.

One of your farming enterprises is artisan meats and charcuterie. How did you learn this skill? We were introduced to charcuterie by a vendor at one of the farmers markets we attended. Doug instantly fell in love with the product(s). The more we investigated and sampled, the more we learned how aligned the old world arts of Charcuterie and Salumi were with our heritage focus. As we approached charcuterie firms as an outlet for whole animal sales, we also choose to partner up to learn more about this product line. As we have had charcuterie made product for us from our Berkshire hogs, we have expanded our knowledge greatly. We now possess a much deeper understanding of how to manage and handle, preserve and package, educate and represent the product as we bring this product line to our market.

We have studied the art, reading broadly, taken classes, sampled charcuterie, and worked with these charcuterie experts learning this craft. We are now experimenting making small batches, personal use only, of charcuterie as we perfect our skills.

What regulatory issues did you have to navigate to produce and sell artisan meats? Our charcuterie is being made by a third party for us. The biggest regulatory issue is needing a commercial kitchen to make this product, which we do not have on the farm. We are currently exploring how to best meet the regulatory issues to begin making the charcuterie ourselves.

If starting over again on the path to self-sufficiency, what would you do differently? I find a "do it over again" a dangerous question. While there are certainly trials and tribulations, each comes with unparalleled learning. Any deviation would dilute the knowledge and experience we have gained. For instance, we attempted to buy the adjoining farm when it was on the market. In hindsight, we should have closed on that property. However, without the hindsight of knowing our farm would center on pork production, there is simply no way of knowing how valuable that additional woodland would be.

What do you miss about city/urban life...you know, the "real" world? Since we live on the outskirts of the city/urban life, there really is not much we miss. We have the luxury of being close enough to enjoy the amenities, but far enough removed to keep everything at arm's length.

Finally, what advice do you have for someone considering leaving a "real job" to become more self-sufficient? Our approach to commercial farming has been to "go big or go home." Since Lori and I are both in our 50s, we do not have decades to accomplish what we have set out to accomplish. This strategy is based on over a decade of learning about farming. Without this experience base and the support of the ag community, we could not achieve what we have accomplished. Hence, I suggest not biting off more than you can chew. Build a solid base of experience and knowledge by starting one or two enterprises on a small scale. Master these, then scale these up before expanding. Second, become part of your local ag community. There are tremendous resources (read: knowledge, experience, guidance) available for both the beginning farmer and the experienced farmer.

TRACTOR OR EQUIPMENT DEALER

Perhaps you would like to sell a small amount of farm equipment or feed in your area. If it is under-serviced, then you will find opportunities to do so, and get a discount on your tractor to boot.

FARMSTEAD LOTIONS, CANDLES

You will no doubt learn to make lotions, candles, detergents and more for your homestead. If you have the raw materials, such as lard, goat milk, etc., why not make handcrafted skin care products or candles for customers? These products lend themselves to both local markets as well as distant markets via online sales or distributor relationships. As the profiles in this book of both BubbaTanicals and Little Seed Farm illustrate, there is a more value-added opportunity with making lotions, shampoos, soaps and creams that are all natural and free of chemicals.

HANDCRAFTED ARTISANAL SOAP

Making soap is easy to learn. Packaging, marketing, and creating a business that successfully sells soaps… well, that is a different matter. But you can do it and, for many, soap production is a fairly lucrative business. I know of numerous people who successfully centered their homestead on income from soap making. Can you be one of them? In chapter one I shared a profile of Brian and Laura Tant who are making soap part-time at BubbaTanicals, but now I would like to share the story of a wonderful couple who up and left New York city for full-time farming in the hills of Tennessee. I first met James and Eileen Ray when they flew down from New York to our farm in Georgia to attend one of our farm schools along with 24 other hopeful farmsteaders. After just a few moments with them it was immediately apparent that they not only had the dream of living a more self-sufficient life, but that they would realize that dream. In three short years, they have traded the orderly chaos of taxis creeping steadily through New York City for disorderly goats meandering through fields in rural Tenneesee, learning along the way to make exceptional soap and cheese. It has been a joy to witness the birth of Little Seed Farm and I am proud to share their story with you.

PROFILE # 16

"Bringing the pace of city life to the country can only produce disaster, so get ready to slow down."

– James Ray

Who: James & Eileen Ray, LittleSeedFarm.com

Where: Lebanon, Tennessee (just outside Nashville)

Homestead/Farm Highlights: We farm an 84 acre parcel of land in Middle Tennessee, surrounded by the Cedars of Lebanon State Park. Our focus is goat dairying, with over 30 goats rotationally grazing our 35 acres of pasture. Ossabaw Island Hogs live in our woodlands and consume the whey leftover from our cheesemaking operation. Three livestock guardian dogs protect it all.

What were your "real jobs" before and what inspired (or scared) you into pursuing a more self-sufficient lifestyle? We worked "burnout" jobs in New York City. James worked in finance as an investment analyst, while Eileen worked as a fashion designer.

When leaving your "real jobs" in the city what was the most challenging thing about taking the leap to your new life? Leaving the security of a steady income was definitely one of the hardest parts. Once you start providing your own income, paying your own insurance, etc., it really hits home and you realize how difficult it is to make a living as a full-time farmer. In addition, having no background in farming is very challenging from an animal husbandry standpoint. Our priority has always been our animals' happiness and health. Having so many living beings under your care is a huge responsibility, and cannot be taken lightly.

What are your sources of income now? For the first two years James worked an off-farm job to help get the farm started. As the business grew he was able to quit his job and farm with Eileen full time. The primary source of income on the farm is the sale of goat's milk soap and other skincare products. In addition, we operate a raw milk cheese share where members receive a different cheese each week, similar to a CSA.

How do you sell your products and how did you build a customer base? Did you have marketing backgrounds? The soap and skincare products are distributed primarily via wholesale, but we also do farmers markets, festivals, and offer all our products online. The cheese is distributed directly to shareholders at farmers markets in Nashville.

What inspired you to offer soap as your primary product? Are the profit margins in soap higher than in other farmstead enterprises? Soap really took on a life of its own. We never intended to focus primarily on soap production, but as demand continued to grow we decided to keep up and make soap a cornerstone of Little Seed Farm's product offering. The scalability of soap made it appealing as a farmstead business. One person can produce tens of thousands of bars of soap, whereas many other farm enterprises would require additional labor for such large volumes. As a value-added product, the profit margins for soap tend to be higher than certain other farm products.

How did you learn the art of soap making, and how does producing and selling soap differ from simply making soap for your own use? We were entirely self-taught when it comes to soap making. Initially, we started making soap for ourselves and our family. As we used the soap and realized its benefits it became apparent that selling the soap was a viable option. Homemade soap is so much more moisturizing and enjoyable to use that it seemed crazy to us that more people were not using it.

Producing soap in large volumes requires a lot more than making it for one's personal use. For one, large-scale production equipment is required for increased production. A separate facility outside the home is also a plus. Beyond that, branding, packaging, and distributing is a huge factor in bringing a soap product to market.

Starting a business for the first time can be scary. How did you figure out the rules and regulatory issues for selling soap, cheese, etc? Research. We spent an inordinate amount of time speaking with other farmers, various regulatory bodies, lawyers, and so forth to determine what was allowed and what was not. The Internet and books help to some degree, but actually getting in front of other human beings was the biggest help.

If starting over what would you do differently? Honestly, we could not have asked for a better start. Our expectation was for things to pan out worse than they actually have. Going into farming we were very afraid of losing animals and not being able to properly care for them. Thus far we have been fortunate to have lost very few animals.

As far as the business goes, growth from product sales has exceeded all expectations and we are thrilled to be full-time farming after just a couple years of getting started. Maybe it sounds silly or unrealistic, but we would not change a thing.

Finally, what advice do you have for someone considering leaving a "real job" to pursue a more self-sufficient lifestyle? It is hard, hard work. While it is immensely enjoyable and rewarding, we also work 12 to 18 hours per day nearly every day of the week. With dairy farming you rarely have a break, and when you add a manufacturing business such as soap or cheese, you have little time to rest. Our advice would be to start slowly and make sure you love what you are doing and do not mind it literally taking over your life. If you are a small business, you will not be able to travel frequently and your income will be abysmal. With larger scale those things may change and you may be able to hire employees, but if you are trying to keep it as a "homestead" operation, be prepared to work well beyond "full-time." The only additional advice would be to have patience. There is nothing the animals and Mother Nature have taught us more than patience. Rushing the natural world results in massive problems. Bringing the pace of city life to the country can only produce disaster, so get ready to slow down. That is what it is all about anyway, right?

SEWING/KNITTING

There was a time when virtually every household had a sewing machine and one or more household inhabitants was skilled at sewing and mending. In fact, I still have the clear recollection of my grandmother rhythmically sewing away on her treadle sewing machine. Often, she would get together with other ladies and they would piece together beautiful quilts. They did not call them "vintage" or "handmade," but of course they would be considered that now, and there are many people today with disposable incomes (perhaps you are one of them) who long for this connection to the past. They think little of plunking down a few hundred dollars for something truly unique. And, while grandma would have had a diffcult time selling her quilt to anyone (since everyone could make one), you can use marketplaces such as Etsy to sell worldwide! Oh, if grandma could see us now! You could also consider selling supplies such as wool or yarn, or you could add value by sewing bags, aprons, cloth diapers, and more.

I hope some of these ideas got you thinking about how you can sell products and make a good living off your farm or homestead, but I bet you know of even more ways! Many products and skills I have discussed are small scale and tug more at the homesteader›s heart. Some, such as retail meats, cured meats and commercial cheesemaking speak more to those interested in farming as a business. Which is right for you? It depends greatly on how you answer the questions posed earlier in this book. Namely, how much money do you need to make? But it also depends on how ambitious you are and how much energy you have. These are issues for you to ponder.

Chapter Five
Save Money as a Homesteader

"A penny saved is a penny earned."

— Benjamin Franklin

In the first chapter, I mentioned often hearing the question, "Can you make a living as a farmer, prepper, or homesteader?" Sometimes the question is more revealing than any answer I could provide, for it fails to consider one of the most obvious benefits of homesteading: homesteaders have far more opportunities to eliminate or reduce expenses than most consumers do.

Here are 30 great tips to save you lots of money on your homesteading adventure.

1. **Buy cheap stuff** - How? For one, purchase only used things, such as used automobiles, clothes, and toys from Goodwill or thrift stores. Also, make a habit of going to farm auctions where you can find anything and everything farm related for next to nothing. Often, you will see brand new merchandise being sold in liquidation sales by big box landscape and home improvement stores.

2. **Make your own clothes** - Learn to knit, sew, and/or crochet. Mend clothes before buying new ones. Even if that "new" pair of jeans comes from a thrift store, it still costs money and takes fuel to get there.

3. **Buy cheap land** – If you are interested in using your skills rather than the land to produce income, then consider less fertile land that you can get at a steep discount.

4. **Barter construction labor** - If you are handy as a carpenter or skilled in other ways, barter those services for what you need. If you are not handy but have a woodlot, cut and barter your firewood for items or skills you need. In both cases, Craigslist can be a useful tool for finding bartering partners.

5. **Do it yourself** - Sure, this means painting your own home, changing your own oil, mowing your own grass, etc. but it also means being creative in making things that you want or need. For example, my wife is wonderful at making all the games and educational props we use to homeschool our daughter, meaning we purchase very little in that area. She also studies herbalism and makes medicinal tinctures from herbs we grow as well as our soaps, salves, lotions, and shampoos. When we want a greenhouse to start plants or a custom playhouse for our daughter, we build them ourselves. In fact, a couple of years ago, we wanted a new island for our kitchen. Rather than buy one for hundreds or thousands of dollars, my wife and I made one for less than $25 using discarded pallets and a piece of plywood. See picture below!

A homemade kitchen island

6. **Limit food shopping** - Grow as much food yourself as you can, especially meats, vegetables, and fruits. If you must shop, shop for ingredients with which to MAKE food, and purchase bulk grains for long-term storage. Buy bulk dried beans at a fraction of the cost of canned beans and learn to can them yourself in a pressure canner.

7. **Visit an LDS Cannery** - Regardless of your religious views and affiliation, the Church of Jesus Christ Latter Day Saints provides dozens of home storage center locations throughout the country where you can purchase bulk items at prices far below wholesale. Yep, you can purchase them at cost and they will even show you how to can them in the storage center in #10 cans so the food will last 20 years or more! Commonly stocked foods include all sorts of beans, rice, wheat, oats, sugar, flour, potato flakes, pasta, apple slices, and more. If you cannot make it to a location, you can even order from the store.lds.org website and they will ship to you at very low cost!

8. **Swap classes** - If you offer classes (such as on cheesemaking, butchering, etc.), consider trading a class spot to someone who teaches things you would like to learn (survival skills, etc.). This will help you to acquire the knowledge you seek without laying out cash.

9. **Beat inflation with the prepper mindset** - How? Purchase large quantities of bulk food at buying clubs and learn to properly store them for the long term. Write the prices you paid on containers and compare them a couple of years later to current prices. The food inflation you see will not affect you since you purchased at the lower cost, giving you the same financial gain as you would realize if your stock portfolio went up, except for one critical difference; unlike your stock portfolio, you do not have to pay taxes on your gain vs. inflation!

10. **Start your own vegetables from seeds** - Do not buy transplants when, for a fraction of the cost, you can start your own seeds and learn a great skill at the same time. Seeds are cheap; buy plenty and store in your freezer.

11. **Spend money on things that will make you money** – Before spending money on any item, ask yourself if the purchase will mean additional expenses (such as maintenance) or if it will produce passive income for you. For example, purchasing livestock that will gleefully breed and reproduce will reward you with a continual supply of food (saving you lots of money) or earn you income, or both, for your family.

12. **Make your own alcohol** - If you do not drink, skip this one, but the rest of us know how expensive good wine can be. Before homesteading, I often purchased decent bottles of wine. Today I most often drink mead, made from our honey and water, both free for the taking, and sometimes make wine from blackberries or other free fruits of the land. The bottles are reused so the cost of social lubrication on the homestead is dramatically less than it is at the suburban bar.

13. **Cut your own hair** - Self explanatory. The bigger your family, the more cash you can start pocketing.

14. **Discount dental care** - If you live relatively close to one, participate in a dental implant clinic/program held at a school of dentistry where recently graduated dentistry school students look to gain experience by performing dental implant procedures, supervised by experienced dentists or dental surgeons, of course. If you can get into one you can save thousands!

15. **Ditch your gym membership** - Chop firewood, take long pasture walks, hoist bags of feed and practice yoga in front of your chickens.

16. **Keep your clunker** - There was a time in my life when I took pride in purchasing a new car every couple of years. Yes, though it embarrasses me now, I was once a poster child for the Fed's weapons of mass consumption campaign. Today, I am a recovering consumer; my truck has a replaced transmission, over 250,000 miles on it and I am determined to make it to the half million mile mark!

17. **Ditch Internet service** - I know, you cannot live without it and, truth be told, I suspect I cannot either. But that does not mean we have to pay for it. Instead, when you do make your trips to town, plan to spend time at places with free wi-fi. Plunk down a couple of bucks at the same time for coffee if you can afford it. Otherwise, go to the library for free wi-fi. While you are there, check out some free books to read when you are back home. After all, you will need something to do now you are unplugged!

18. **Do not make frivolous trips** - Plan and organize travel since you will likely be farther away from your destinations. Also, do not make trips to have your oil changed or car washed. Do those yourself and save even more money.

19. **Ditch your TV** - The average cable subscriber spends more than $1,500 per year for cable service and associated fees. Instead, go old school and install an antenna to get FREE HDTV!

20. **When you do spend, pay for quality** - But pay cash or, better yet, barter! Just buy the best item you can once for a lifetime rather than purchasing the same cheaply made item over and over.

21. **Make your own gifts** - Be honest, which gift is likely to be more treasured for a lifetime: something made of plastic and bought with cash or something handmade by you specifically

for the recipient? In our case, we long ago began making most of our own Christmas gifts as well as those for birthdays, anniversaries and so on. Of course, this does not mean that you must never again "buy" something, for we certainly do buy manufactured goods, but it does mean looking for opportunities to make something special yourself. Both you and the recipient will feel good about it and you will save money to boot.

22. **Hunt and fish** - Learn to hunt and fish so you can keep an endless supply of free meat for your family.

23. **Feed your dogs for free** - Livestock guardian dogs can be expected to eat 50 to 60 pounds of high-quality food per month. This is for each dog and some homesteaders have several. We have five, so that is at least 250 pounds per month of feed. Depending on the quality of feed it is reasonable to expect the feed costs to be at least $300 per year per dog. In our case, that is $1,500. So how can you feed them for free? Well, if you can hunt and live in an area (as we do) where deer populations grow essentially uncontrolled, consider harvesting more deer than your family needs as a free and much more nutritious source of food for your livestock dogs! This is much more akin to a natural diet for them than anything you could buy in a store. Also, if you butcher animals on your farm, the dogs will be grateful for any chicken and pig feet, entrails, etc. that you may not want.

24. **Make your own cleaning products** - Making soap, shampoo, and lotion is easy. Use your own beeswax or buy in bulk at soapgoods.com and you can save a bundle.

25. **Grow your own medicine** - As you learn about medicinal herbs, you will learn that you can grow and harvest many plants and turn them into medicines to preserve your family's health rather than taking the modern approach of simply

curing symptoms.

26. **Enter writing contests** - If you have the interest, seek and enter writing contests such as the one on SurvivalBlog.com. This contest runs continually and prizes can be worth many thousands of dollars! The good news is that not only will the prizes be items/skills that you value, but your newfound knowledge and experience makes you a perfectly qualified contributing author! And if you think the prizes are not real or the contest is fixed, think again. I entered the contest early in 2014 and won first prize, valued at about $5,000! Those were valuable items to us as homesteaders, saving us a lot of money. You too could win... but only if you enter.

27. **Homeschool** - Perhaps you can give your children a better education while saving money on transportation to school at a minimum or, for even more savings, by forgoing private school tuition.

28. **Take vacations for virtually nothing** - How? Check out sites such as HomeExchange.com to find ways to swap your dream location for someone else's so you can both get away from it all!

29. **Choose free entertainment** - Rural towns offer a host of free events throughout the year that can provide you and your family with an entertaining diversion from the farm. These events include movies in the park, concerts, farm days, and more. Check out listings in your local newspaper or in tourism guides.

30. **Build or buy a smaller house** - In the 1950s a typical American home was approximately 1,100 square feet and had one bathroom. To make matters worse, the average family size was much larger back then, making it common for two or three children to share a bedroom. Compare

that to 2012 in which, according to the Census Bureau, the median home in the U.S. average was 2,306 square feet! This is far more than most people need, and the excess space increases the tax burden, drives up heating and cooling costs, and requires more time to clean. If you find yourself with a home that is too big, consider renting out rooms to generate some income. Better yet, live debt free in a tiny house or travel trailer! For inspiration, check out the profile below on Kerri Fivecoat-Campbell. Unlike most of us, she embraced living in a house smaller than some family rooms!

PROFILE # 17

> "My husband had worked 24 years for a company that was being sold and we knew he might lose his job."
>
> – Kerri Fivecoat-Campbell

Who: Kerri Fivecoat-Campbell and Dale Campbell, founder of livinglargeinourlittlehouse.com

Where: Ozark Mountains, Arkansas

What was your "real job" prior to breaking away to become more self-sufficient? I ran a freelance writing business, writing for major metropolitan newspapers for 9 years. Prior to that, I worked in consumer credit for one of the largest banks in the country.

What inspired you to start down the road to becoming more self-sufficient? My mother passed away in February 2007 and for me, it was painful driving by our childhood homes. We had never lived more than two miles from those homes and decided we needed a change. My husband had worked 24 years for a company that was being sold and we knew he might lose his job. We had a lake home we built in 2003 and decided to move.

Homestead/Farm Highlights: We have nearly 10 acres of wooded property in the beautiful Ozark Mountains. In the summer, we grow a small container garden. We buy locally sourced food from our town's natural food store. Our Little House has a well, which allows us not to have to rely on municipal water. We also heat our home exclusively with a wood stove and we have enough woods to source from felled trees. My husband has a garage and is a mechanic by trade, so he could work from home, but he chooses to work at a company where we can get healthcare coverage. I have a 320-foot writer's studio that allows me to work from home and care for our five recycled (rescue) dogs.

What are your income streams? I am a writer. My husband is a mechanic at a large manufacturer in town.

If starting over, what would you do differently? Our 480-square-foot Little House was not meant to be a full-time residence. Although we had the foresight to build it as a fully functioning home, it is too small to house two heirloom pieces of furniture I wanted to keep. I would make it just a bit bigger at 600 square feet, raise the ceiling for more depth and to make it feel bigger, and install solar panels to be off grid.

How hard was it, really, when you first moved into a tiny cabin? I mean, did you not have too much stuff? LOL. Yes and we still are trying to rid our lives of the clutter. We have a storage building and are eliminating little by little.

What do you miss about city/urban life...you know, the "real" world? At first, we missed good restaurants and the choice of things to do in the winter. We are outdoors people, so the good weather months, typically March to November, are great for us. We boat and fish, hike, 4-wheel. However, the winters are a killer. I particularly miss concerts and cultural events (theater and museums), movie theaters. Of course, we miss our friends.

What advice do you have for someone considering leaving a "real job" to become more self-sufficient? Save, save, and save. The recession hit us just a year after our move and it became apparent very quickly that we did not have enough savings to cover an 18-month lay off for my husband.

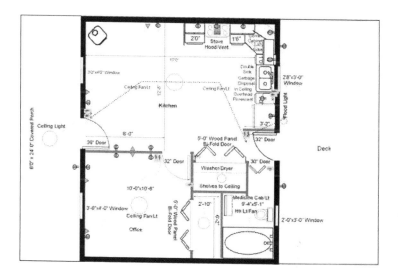

Chapter Six
Personalize Your Farmstead Business Plan

"There are two spiritual dangers in not owning a farm.
One is the danger of supposing that breakfast
comes from the grocery, and the other that heat comes from
the furnace."
— Aldo Leopold

By this point, I have exposed you to numerous ways you can produce income from a home-based business. I do not know about you, but knowing these income streams are available gives me a lot of comfort!

People new to homesteading, or entrepreneurial life in general, are often nervous, if not downright scared, about the prospects of not having a comfortable and secure paycheck coming in each week. I was like that once, but I let go of Linus's blanket a long time ago. I am not so old that I cannot remember how emotionally trying (and exhilarating) the transition was, so I will not lie about that. What I will say is that when you do make that transition and learn how to generate income for yourself, you will never again worry about being laid off, how your employer is doing or if you will have money in retirement. You will make the life you want for yourself and no one will be there to deny you the pay raise if you want it, or more time off when you need it, although getting both would be the ultimate triumph!

So far this book has described many life choices to address in preparing for life as a self-sufficient homesteader. It has described dozens of ways you can make money living your dream life, so I suppose it is fitting that the book ends with the call for you to make decisions about what income opportunities are most appealing to you.

The author and his wife Liz, loving life in the country

At the risk of repeating myself, I wish to reiterate that if you live cheaply and lightly, then you do not have to generate very much income. You may be aware that food prices have been steadily escalating and will likely continue to do so for many years. By producing much of what you now pay to consume you will in effect increase your wealth. You will most certainly increase your self-reliance and security. This means you can give up on the modern mantra of chasing more and more money and enjoy more quality time that costs next to nothing. Some people, however, will want to maximize income so they can enjoy travel, pay medical or education expenses or just watch the money grow. We each must decide for ourselves exactly what we want. The best advice I can give to you is this:

Do what you love so you will love what you do!

LIFESTYLE CONSIDERATIONS FOR CHOOSING A HOMESTEAD BUSINESS

Most of the income-generating ideas presented thus far assume you will be pursuing a self-sufficient lifestyle on a homestead, but some, such as monetized blogging, freelancing, etc., do not. You could start earning income through those online ventures from a tiny apartment in the most densely populated city while preparing yourself for the leap to self-sufficiency. These businesses are wonderful in the sense that the income stream is portable! When you move, you can take the online revenue stream with you to the farm, ranch, or the proverbial beach. Regardless of which one (or more) of the income-producing enterprises appeals to you, it is important that you fully consider the lifestyle considerations of that choice prior to jumping in.

For instance, I have hands-on experience with numerous farming enterprises. For the most part I love them all, but the demands they place on your lifestyle vary greatly. Assume for a moment that you are drawn to cheesemaking, as I am, but are trying to decide between the large investment required for farmstead cheesemaking vs. the more modest investment in artisanal cheesemaking. Here are questions you may want to answer to make the best choice for you.

LIFESTYLE CONSIDERATIONS OF ARTISANAL VS. FARMSTEAD CHEESEMAKING

- How often do you want to make cheese? (With farmstead you have to make cheese every couple of days at least, but with artisanal, you could take time off from cheesemaking, since you only make cheese when you purchase milk).
- Do you know how to make cheese?
- How much cheese do you want/need to sell to make ends meet, financially?
- Do you know how to run a business?
- Do you want to milk animals every day and have greater control/potentially higher profits (farmstead), or do you want

to buy milk and have more flexibility but loss of control/potentially reduced profits (artisanal)?

- Are you prepared to pull calves/lambs and help with the birthing process if needed?
- Are you skilled at marketing and branding so that you may successfully build a loyal customer base?
- Are you comfortable working entrepreneurially (independently) and without the safety net of company health care, pension plans, 401K, ability to call in sick and easily schedule vacations, etc.?
- If you are interested in farmstead cheese, do you want to milk year round or seasonally? If seasonal, will you need to generate income in the "off" months? If so, how will you do this?
- How much are you willing to invest? Farmstead requires much more, both up front and ongoing.
- Is there something unique you can bring to market?
- Are you ready for your life and work to become inseparable?
- Are you willing to do the same thing, every day, every year?

You can apply this list or a similar list of questions to any enterprise you are considering. If it is a new enterprise that you are not familiar with, do not be shy about contacting others who are doing it. Ask them some of these questions and seek their wisdom on the lifestyle considerations of each. The time to think about this is now when you are planning so you do not become trapped later on.

PERSONALIZING YOUR FARMSTEAD INCOME PLAN

I have introduced you to four categorical ways that you can achieve profitability on your farmstead (land, skills, products) along with ways to save money by homesteading. Within each category are dozens of choices. One way to help you to decide what is right for you is to map out the monthly cash flow implications of each decision. Even if you are very frugal, it is likely that you will have at least some expenses each month. Therefore, you will need cash regularly, either earned in the month it is needed or a surplus from prior earnings. So when thinking about income opportunities, I find it helpful to visualize how money flows in monthly. To aid you with that, take a look at the following income-calendar tool:

Farmstead Income Calendar Example

Income Enterprise	Income Category	Jan	Feb	Mar	Apr	May	Jun	Jul	Aug	Sep	Oct	Nov	Dec
INCOME													
Farm Stays	LAND					$	$	$	$	$	$		
Cheese Classes	SKILLS	$	$	$	$								
Artisan Cheese	PRODUCT			$	$	$	$						
TOTAL INCOME		$	$	$	$	$	$	$	$	$	$	-	-
EXPENSE													
Farm Stays	LAND					$	$	$	$	$	$	$	
Cheese Classes	SKILLS	$	$	$	$								
Artisan Cheese	PRODUCT	$	$	$	$	$	$						
TOTAL EXPENSE		$	$	$	$	$	$	$	$	$	$	$	$
NET CASH FLOW													
Farm Stays	LAND				$	$	$	$	$	$	$		
Cheese Classes	SKILLS	$	$	$	$							$	
Artisan Cheese	PRODUCT	$	$	$	$	$	$	$	$	$	$		
NET CASH FLOW		$	$	$	$	$	$	$	$	$	$	$	$

Of course the income calendar is NOT a cash flow or income statement, which is much more detailed. Rather, this is simply a visual aid... an income calendar, if you will, to get you thinking about when you could expect to generate income (yea!) and when you would have to spend money (boo!). Ideally the "net" each month and at year-end will be a surplus. If not, there is a problem that you will need to address.

INCOME-CALENDAR EXAMPLE

To tie this income-calendar tool into what you have read so far, I used three examples of income enterprises in this calendar with one coming from each category (land, products, and skills) presented earlier in this book. In the above image I assumed that farm stays would be an income source that the **land** could help generate. Based on a farmstead location in a mid-northern climate, I assumed that the farmstead could generate income in the months of May through October, since the fictional homesteader in my example is using a converted but non-heated barn. However, she would incur expenses in the months April through November, since she will have to prep and close the facilities. Since she will be busy with guests in the summer, income from other sources is not assumed during those months.

In the cooler months, the homesteader uses a quaint, but approved, commercial kitchen to make artisan cheese as a farmstead **product**. She buys milk for this enterprise beginning each January, because she likes to have a lot of free time in November and December for the holidays. That is her lifestyle choice and she knows she needs to accumulate cash throughout the year to afford it.

Since she is making cheese anyway between January and April, she chooses to use her **skills** to offer frequent cheesemaking classes during those months. She ages the cheese from her classes to sell at retail later but is able to augment that revenue by teaching skills while she makes cheese. Her customers are thrilled to cut the curds and learn the magic of cheesemaking and they are eager to buy cheese from her later, so it is a real win-win exchange.

Even though our fictitious homesteader makes cheese in January and February and, therefore, has significant expenses (milk, etc.) during those months, she does not begin realizing income from the raw-milk cheeses until March, as they have to age 60 days or more. Her cheese sales then continue through June and she will have modest costs associated through the entire period, as she has to keep coolers running. By then, the summer guests arriving at the farm stay are happy to purchase her cheeses since they are there, giving her a high-margin distribution path and enhancing the farm-stay experience.

Of course there are several expense items that do not correlate exactly to a specific enterprise, such as taxes to be paid on the entire homestead, home and equipment repairs, fuel, health care, and so on. If you want to plan for this the way most people do, then most of these would be personal expenses and belong in your personal budget, with the homesteading budget replacing a paycheck. The monthly net from the paycheck (after accrued taxes) would have to meet or exceed your personal budget requirements.

MARKETING YOUR FARMSTEAD PRODUCTS

Regardless what products or services you choose to offer from your farmstead, if you are not successful at marketing them, you will not be financially successful. While this is not intended to be a marketing book, I would like to devote a few pages to go-to-market approaches and publicity that may help you to determine the path that is best for you.

Here are the typical go-to-market options for common farmstead products such as meat, dairy, eggs, fruit and vegetables, but they apply equally to most physical things you are likely to sell.

Farmers Markets/Festivals (Direct Sales to Consumers)

Pros - High profit margin since you are capturing 100 percent of the retail value. You also gain immediate and direct customer feedback, have the ability to capture email and build a marketable base of loyal customers, and can sell cheese by the pound and ensure you are paid for 100 percent of the wheel

Cons - Very time consuming, and you can only be at so many places at once; markets are becoming more difficult to get into, some requiring certification (organic, etc.), and sales will be low in poor weather

Online/Mail Order (Direct Sales to Consumers)

<u>Pros</u> - High profit margin, ability to sell nationwide; much greater marketing ability

<u>Cons</u> - Need to invest in shipping boxes/insulators/cooling packs, transport to shipping centers, slice and wrap cheeses if made from larger wheels (since you sell by fixed price online, you will lose if your slice is larger than you advertised); lots of customer service required; marketing "look and feel" becomes much more important

On-Farm store (Direct Sales to Consumers)

<u>Pros</u> - All the pros of farmers markets/festivals, plus you do not have to leave the comfort of your home; could be coupled with agri-tourism to generate additional income

<u>Cons</u> - If your store is open often (to capture more potential sales), you always need to be there...so you are really always "on call"

Wholesale to Restaurants/Retailers

<u>Pros</u> - Ability to sell whole/multiple wheels; cachet of being on finer menus and endorsed by leading chefs can enhance your brand; you do not have to invest heavily in marketing

<u>Cons</u> - Lower (but good) profit margins as you have to price the cheese approximately 40 percent less than retail; if you work with larger restaurants, you could put too many of your eggs in one basket; you may still have to ship cheese depending on where you want to sell; loss of direct customer contact

Distributors

<u>Pros</u> - Easiest method; distributors often pick up at farm with refrigerated vehicles; orders can be very large and very frequent; very little time needed on your part for customer service; distributors can cover nationwide; may be best option if you value lifestyle/

time over maximizing income

<u>Cons</u> - Lowest profit margin; very little customer control

Beyond these go-to-market options, you will still need to invest in your own branding. This means logo design, excellent web presence consistent with your desired image, social media presence to enhance awareness and drive traffic to your chosen distribution paths, and so on.

Method	Pros	Cons
Distributor	1. Broad delivery handled for you 2. Has a buyer database 3. Delivery done for you 4. May sell "hard to sell" items	1. Lower price 2. No control of customer relationship 3. Brand risk 4. Risk (may switch to other farms)
Restaurant	1. Exposure/Endorsement 2. Volume 3. Predictability	1. Risk (eggs in one basket) 2. Lower price 3. Demanding
Direct to Customer	1. Ownership of customers 2. Diversification of revenue 3. Maximum price 4. Ability to target market offerings	1. Must be able to sell/market 2. Most labor intensive 3. Requires more capital 4. Requires more specialized skills

GETTING PUBLICITY FOR YOUR FARMSTEAD OPERATION

If one of your goals is to create a brand and sell your farmstead products, services or events, I suspect you will soon create your own brochures, website, and social media pages. Beyond that there is one powerful marketing tool that can really create exposure for you, if that is what you want. That is the power of publicity.

In our first few years on the farm we received, and benefited from, the following publicity:

- Feature story (twice) in the Atlanta Journal-Constitution (AJC)
- Feature story in The New York Times
- Appeared in a story that featured our farm on RFDTV
- Appeared live on Fox & Friends
- Profiled on an NPR blog
- Interviewed in an NPR affiliate radio segment
- Featured in a CNN segment story on our farm's meat CSA program
- On the cover of ACRES USA magazine
- Featured in a Southern Living Magazine story on rare-breed Ossabaw Island hogs
- Featured several times in regional papers, including the Athens Banner-Herald
- Profiled in Garden & Gun Magazine
- Our cheese featured on live television on MSNBC's The Morning Joe show
- Numerous other mentions, awards, and articles

Third Annual Made in the South Awards

BY VANESSA GREGORY, ELIZABETH HUTCHISON AND T. EDWARD NICKENS · DECEMBER 2012/JANUARY 2013

Dixie's best in Home, Style + Design, Outdoors, and Food

Winner: Food Category

Nature's Harmony Farm

You cannot buy this free publicity from such reputable sources, nor can you easily duplicate the credible impact that it lends your farmstead business. So how were we so fortunate to earn it, and how can you?

Other than the first article that appeared on our farm (AJC) above, we did not seek any of the publicity. Rather, we were contacted directly by each organization after they somehow discovered us. In the AJC case, I pitched a simple story idea of the consumer demand for heritage turkeys. Naturally, I pitched this idea in October knowing that the AJC, like most news outlets, would appreciate a new angle on a story they had to cover every year, Thanksgiving. And therein lies the "secret," if there is one, to garnering publicity; having a story that is not about your needs, but relevant and intriguing for the media source's readers, viewers, and listeners.

Soon after the AJC article appeared, we were contacted by an NPR outlet to do a radio segment on our heritage turkeys, but also our broader farm as well. A few months later I received an email from a New York Times reporter asking to visit us to do a feature story. We were as shocked by that as anyone, but who were we to question what the New York Times deemed to be a story of interest to its readers.

Most of these and later media requests came, I suspect, as a result of our frequent blog articles. In these articles we described what we were doing on the farm (many of the articles are presented in *The Accidental Farmers*) including our meat CSA, butchering classes, offering heritage turkeys, raising rare Ossabaw Island pigs and so on. After such reputable sources as CNN, The New York Times, NPR and Fox News covered us, they provided links to our website, which, of course, increased our rankings and visibility on search engines and created a snowball effect.

Beyond pitching the initial story to the AJC, we entered our cheeses into a number of competitions. One of these was the annual Made in the South competition sponsored by Garden & Gun Magazine, which currently has a total audience of over 1.1 million readers with an average household income of well over $300,000. To our great surprise, we won first place in the food category the only year we entered. That recognition resulted in a lot of exposure for

us, and we received a secondary kick when the magazine decided to feature our cheese on MSNBC's Morning Joe show, a publicity spot they negotiated.

What publicity lessons can you take from our experiences? Here are a few ideas IF you would like to increase publicity exposure:

1. Blog, and blog frequently.

2. When you write your articles pay careful attention to A) the article title, B) the keywords in the article, and C) effective incorporation of images with alt tags. When determining the best blog titles and keywords, imagine what someone may be searching for. For example, is it more likely that someone will type "hog butchering class in Georgia" in a search box or "what we did on the farm this weekend"? If you think the former, then that should be your title AND it

should be part of the URL. Take the same care when creating your navigation menu. After all, how many consumers will type in the phrase "about us"?

3. If you produce a product that can be entered into a competition, do so if you would like increased exposure. Seek out those competitions and enter... you never know!

4. When speaking with reporters, pay careful attention to what THEY see as the story angle. Why do they want to feature your farm or your products? Once you understand the angle you can, and should, spin your narrative around that. You and the reporter are on the same team; you both want to create a compelling story that consumers will respond to.

5. Be careful what you wish for. You just may find that others are interested in what you are doing and you may constantly be swamped by requests. For example, partly as a result of the media exposure, we found ourselves inundated with emails, tour requests, invitations to speaking engagements, additional interview requests and so on. Again, decide in advance how much of your life you want to share with the media and others.

While we did desire and appreciate the initial exposure we received, we neither sought nor wanted much of the later publicity that came our way. At some point, we felt we were sacrificing too much of our private lives, so after our fifth year of farming we decided to go a bit undercover, if you will, to avoid additional media requests. We took our blog down so it would stop driving inquiries to us, ceased recording podcasts and took those down for the same reasons and reworked our website to simply describe what we offer, and no more. Predictably, these actions made us less visible, which was our goal. Publicity is a wonderful way to gain exposure for your business, but as I indicated in *The Accidental Farmers,* we never moved "out here" to create a business that consumed us. We moved here for the lifestyle and we continue to strive to find that perfect balance of having "just enough" business to meet our financial self-sufficiency goals. No more, no less.

OTHER THOUGHTS ON HOMESTEAD INCOME

Before closing this chapter let me offer a few tips to consider when making choices about the enterprises you pursue.

- Consider generating scalable income for one of your enterprises that does not depend on your immediate labor, for what if you are injured or on vacation? For example, if you are teaching a class, you only get paid if you are there to teach it, but if you later write a book to share your knowledge (or story) it can sell online while you are collecting eggs… or teaching a class!

- Remember, the lowest-cost and easiest-to-start enterprise for you is also the lowest cost and easiest to start for competitors, so strive to create a revenue stream that is buffered. Many farmsteaders begin with pastured poultry and chicken tractors or by selling a few vegetables. Make no mistake, there is a market for it, but it may become competitive in your market overnight so you will want a Plan B.

- Think of offerings as either meeting an absolute necessity (people will always need to eat) or a discretionary one (maybe the kids do not need to go to farm camp in a bad economy). The ideal model is to have offerings that allow you to capture discretionary dollars in normal/good times as well as core necessity dollars in all times. In the above income-calendar example, I would expect farm stays to decline significantly in a financial crisis… unless the operator specifically targeted the wealthy, who tend to have discretionary income in any economy. If she did not target them, what would our homesteader do in that case with so much income loss over several months?

- Value-added and costly products can work exceptionally well in good times but may suffer in tougher economic conditions. As a homesteader you will become increasingly isolated from macro economic conditions but, ironically, you will need to be more attuned to the economy since it will greatly affect your customers.

- Remember the seasons… what is needed when? And determine if you have consistent income. If you raise turkeys, you will have energy costs in spring (brooding) and feed costs for five or six months before getting paid in November. Of course you could improve this example by hatching lots of eggs and selling day-old turkey poults in the early months to generate income that would cover your feed bills for the turkeys you grow out for Thanksgiving. Just know the timing of cash in/out and plan for it. Businesses often fail not because they are not profitable on a net margin basis, but because they run out of cash. This is a very important distinction to understand for the two are not the same thing. Cash is everything for small businesses and remember that profitable farming/homesteading **IS A SMALL BUSINESS**. Operate it as such.

- What can you do right away vs. later? Good vegetable production from gardens may take years of building good soil and learning to deal with pests, but you could breed and sell small livestock right away to build cash until your soil was in shape. Alternatively, if you have the skills, you could teach classes immediately.

- Think about shelf life… you need a market for your veggies before you grow them or you risk loss. Conversely, frozen meats last months, but you will need to PLAN to handle the energy costs to store them.

- Whatever you do, you must THINK AND REMAIN SMALL if you want to homestead. Otherwise, you are not a homesteader… you are a farmer, which is okay as long as that is what you want. Small is subjective, of course, but the goal is to earn what you need to live your dream life, right? For example, Polyface Farm, a highly respected and well-known example of what is possible with sustainable farming, is often perceived as a small family farm, but owner Joel Salatin has reported sales of approximately $2 million per year. Other pasture-based farming operations are considerably larger than that. Operating at that scale requires a minimum of 15 to 20 people, equipment purchases and maintenance, possibly bank loans, detailed operational planning, customer service reps, online presence and social media administrators, delivery drivers, dealing with the media and so on. Then again, Polyface does a marvelous job of showing what is possible, not only in the area of sustainable farming, but, more relevant to this book, the area of sustainable income production. Does that sound like what you are looking for? Or are you looking for something much smaller and simpler? There is no right answer, but remember the old saying: Be careful what you wish for, because you just might get it. Know what your self-sufficient dream is, wish for it, and then go make it a reality.

OVERLAP ENTERPRISES

One approach that works well for many (including us) is to employ overlapping enterprises for income generation and operational efficiency. I mentioned in the last section the opportunity to overlap raising turkeys for Thanksgiving with selling poults (and even hatching eggs) throughout the year. Here is another example that relates to milking cows (or goats or sheep), which could allow you to:

- Sell fluid milk
- Make cheese

- Use whey from cheesemaking as an input for pork production or soap making
- Sell grass-fed beef (dairy steers)
- Teach classes on cheese and soap making, or even other homestead skills such as bread making

A cheesemaking class at Nature's Harmony Farm

In the above example, what is the primary source of income? Is it fluid raw milk? Cheese? Whey-fed pork? Grass-fed beef? Classes? All of the above? And, what is the whey? Is it a waste product for the cheese operation or is it a raw material/input for the pork and soap making businesses? The operator can pick and choose which income streams to emphasize in order to live their homestead dream. As you can probably guess, it is possible to build a rather large farming operation if someone has the energy and passion to do so, and it is equally possible to keep it small, quaint, and more consistent with the idyllic homestead.

For another inspiring example of how a couple realized their dream, take a look at an inspiring story of someone making a living off the land.

PROFILE # 18

"If you do not love your "real job" and think you might love being more self-sufficient and creating a business out of it, you should do it!"

– Lindsey Aparicio

Who: Lindsey and Herbert Aparicio, The Goat Cheese Lady (thegoatcheeselady.com)

Where: Colorado Springs, Colorado

What was your "real job" prior to breaking away to become more self-sufficient? I was an Occupational Therapist. Herbert was a social worker. In 2004, our first son was born and I did not want to return to work as an OT. I have always been entrepreneurial, and, while still in our "city house," Herbert quit his job (and I never went back to mine) we started a real estate business fixing up houses, then selling them through our rent-to-own program. We had always known we wanted land, and in 2009, decided if we ever wanted to move, we had better start looking...although we had no intention of moving right away. Three weeks later, we moved into our new house with an unheard-of 1.6 acres, on the beautiful west side of Colorado Springs. The first few years in the real estate business were great...the remaining years were not. However, we now owned a beautiful house with an incredible view that we could no longer afford, unless I went back to work as an Occupational Therapist. Herbert was still working as the contractor, construction worker and project manager for our real estate business, and I did not want to go back to work as an OT, because our youngest son was still in preschool. Again, being entrepreneurial, I decided, since we already had two goats (we had had them for a couple of months), I would start offering cheesemaking and goat milking classes. I thought, perhaps someone would think it just crazy enough to attend. I have taught nearly 1,000 people since then.

What inspired (or scared) you into starting down the road to becoming more self-sufficient? My husband and I have always been "do-it-yourselfers." Early in our marriage, while living in Tacoma, Washington, he introduced me to chickens. We started a small garden. I tried my hand at canning (a whopping four jars of salsa). We lived on half an acre next to a vacant four-acre plot and we got addicted to having land. After moving back to my hometown of Colorado Springs in 2001, we started up a flock of chickens again, and a garden. That is when I read an article in Organic Gardening about all the fertilizers washing down the Mississippi river and causing a dead zone in the Gulf of Mexico, and when we first began gardening organically. After moving to our current house/farm, we got goats. I had been buying the cheapest milk at the grocery store...whatever was on sale, for our (at the time) two-year-old. I looked at the label; it was from Ohio and it rotted three days later. That was when we decided milk in our back yard was much closer than Ohio. Goats fit in the back of the truck, so goats it was. It was not until I started teaching cheesemaking classes later that year (2010) that I even learned the word "homesteading." We were already doing it with chickens, an organic garden, and goats, but we did not realize it was even "a thing." Since then, we have watched many of the movies, YouTube videos, read books and articles and met many, many people who have caused us to decide, year after year, to continue growing as much of our own food as possible, and buying as little food from grocery stores as possible.

Our farm now provides us with eggs, chicken meat, goat meat, milk, cheese, and 50 percent of our vegetables. We buy half a grass-fed and finished beef each year from a local rancher.

Homestead/Farm Highlights? We currently have four Nubian does in milk, 15 laying hens, three remaining out of 45 meat chickens (the other 42 are in the freezer), 20 meat rabbits, solar greenhouse with rocket stove, organic garden watered by timer-controlled drip system, young 25-tree organic orchard planted using a grey-water system and rain-harvesting techniques planted to model a "food forest."

What are your income streams? Teaching on-farm cheesemaking, bread making, goat milk soap and lotion making, goat milking, and urban homesteading classes. Teaching off-site cheesemaking, bread making and goat milk soap and lotion making classes. Selling herd shares through our herd share program (the legal way in Colorado to obtain and provide raw milk). Selling goat milk soap and lotion.

Why did you choose teaching classes as an income route rather than offering more traditional farm products? When we got goats, I only had experience in the medical and real estate fields. I had no idea there even was a food industry, let alone regulations. With my excess milk, I began making and selling cheese to friends and a couple of local food businesses. It was after multiple people asking me… "do not you need a license for that?" that I began to realize there were regulations for selling food. We would need a commercial kitchen, a Grade-A barn and multiple licenses among other things to legally make and sell cheese. That required too much time and investment, so I stopped selling cheese and thought of teaching classes. When I started teaching cheesemaking classes, one of my students explained how to make soap…so I YouTube soap making and began making and selling and teaching classes on making goat milk soap and lotion. People continued to ask for more classes, so I added an advanced cheesemaking class, bread making class, urban homesteading class, goat milking class and kid's class.

How did you learn to make cheese? And soap? My first introduction to cheesemaking was from a friend. She and I made microwave mozzarella with grocery store cow's milk...before we even had goats. Next, I read about how to make homemade cream cheese. The learning continued from there, with lots of reading, YouTube, trial and error, and observing every week the results of my student's cheesemaking in class.

Starting a business for the first time can be scary. How did you market your classes and products to get customers? Do you have a marketing background? My husband and I had invested too much marketing money into our real estate business, so in starting this business, I vowed to spend no money on marketing. I advertised on Craigslist and learned to create and manage a website and blog on wordpress.com for free. The best marketing (and still free!) came from a student early on in my teaching, who enjoyed The Goat Cheesemaking Class so much that she called the local newspaper and the food editor (Teresa Farney) came out to observe a class and write an article. After that, the classes took off! Now (four years later), we spend a little more than nothing on marketing, but it is still very minimal. We market online and (in January, 2015) in print with the Colorado Springs Visitor's Bureau, print and distribute brochures and business cards every now and then, and that is about it.

If starting over again on the path to self-sufficiency, what would you do differently? Nothing. If we had not had all the experiences we have had, we would not be where we are today.

What do you miss about city/urban life...you know, the "real" world? Free weekends.

What advice do you have for someone considering leaving a "real job" to become more self-sufficient? I believe it is important to work doing something you love. If you do not love your "real job" and think you might love being more self-sufficient and creating a business out of it, you should do it! You can always go back to your "real job" if you want to or need to.

FOCUS

I hope what you have read thus far has motivated you, but if the concepts presented here are new and overwhelming, close the book, catch your breath and take a moment. I am confident that the best idea will choose you more than you will choose it, so let it come to you. When it does, focus on it and learn all you can about it through additional reading, research and mentors. Finding the idea you are passionate about is the first step to realizing your homestead business dreams.

THE HOMESTEAD ENTREPRENEUR LIFE PLAN

It is one thing to have a dream of self-sufficiency. It is another thing to act on it. Far too many times in life we find ourselves wishing, dreaming, and wanting, but not acting. Sometimes we go as far as pen to paper (or fingers to keyboard) analysis but never progress beyond that point. We analyze, talk, analyze some more until we are mired in doubt, suffering from incurable paralysis by analysis.

Do not let this happen to you.

To me it is a tragedy that so many people have dreams they never pursue. Perhaps they just are not sure how to start and create some momentum. What they need is some help... a friendly nudge to get them going. If you feel that way, I would like to offer you a simple tool that has worked for me. Perhaps it will work for you as well. I have modified it for our mutual dreams of self-sufficiency and call it the Homestead Entrepreneurial Life Plan (HELP).

Completing the HELP is the first step down the road to self-sufficient entrepreneurship. Yes, earning dependable income from the homestead makes you an entrepreneur, so celebrate and embrace the notion. It is a blueprint that is unique to each individual and allows each person to express what they want and to map out a plan for realizing it. It is easy to create your own HELP in less than an hour by simply following the template.

PERSONALIZED HELP TEMPLATE

To be successful I need a blueprint for my life. My name is _____, today is _____ and I am ready to put my plan into action to start my own homestead business! I want this dream so much I cannot stand staying put! There are several reasons why I want to start my own self-sufficient business but I would have to say my top three reasons are _____, _____ and _____.

As a result of starting my homestead business several good things could result, including _____, _____ and _____. Of course, some unfortunate things may occur, which include _____, _____ and _____, so I must have a plan to avoid them.

Everyone deserves a chance to be happy and fulfilled in life. On a scale of 1-10, with 10 being the highest, I would rate my current quality of life as a _____. I recognize that every day cannot be an ideal "day on the farm," but when I think of the ideal day I would like to have every day, it would include _____ _____.

Speaking of happiness, the things that make me happiest are
_____, _____
and _____. Likewise, the things that
make me unhappiest are _____,
_____and_____.

We all have different experiences. Through my work experiences,
I have acquired several skills. My three strongest skills are
_____, _____
and _____. Of course, like all people,
I have areas where I need to improve my business skills, and these
include _____, _____
and _____. I can compensate for these
shortcomings by_____.

We all need role models, and in the area of living a successful, self-
sufficient life, the people I know or know of whom I admire are
_____, _____
and _____. We all have a value system, and
these people possess values that are important to me, especially the values
of _____, _____
and _____. I will embody these values in my
homesteading business.

I am anxious to transition to a self-sufficient life immediately, but I
recognize that I have to be ready first. Right now, I feel as if I am being held
back from taking the leap due to _____,
_____ and _____.
And, I have responsibilities, with my biggest obligations being
_____, _____ and
_____. If only I did not have them! But I
do, and truthfully, I know that everyone has obstacles and barriers that
stand between them and their dreams. I refuse to use this as an excuse!

In terms of financial resources, I have savings of $_____. I am not sure how I will make it work, but many others have found a way to transition to a self-sufficient life. I will find a way.

Until now, I have been wishing that I had my own homestead, but I realize that wishes are not goals. My goal is to have a homestead that generates income, so here is what I will do to achieve that starting right now:

1. I will share this plan with someone I trust who will witness it. This represents a life-changing event for me that will also affect others and I want and need support.

2. I will decide NOW to start my homesteading business. A skydiver practices and decides to jump well before they enter the plane so that when they get to the door, they just go. I will take that same approach and I am fully resolved to taking the leap. If necessary I will find mentors so that I can build my knowledge and confidence.

3. I will prepare a simple, two-page plan that defines what my homestead business will be, what customers I will target, what I will offer, how much money I need and what resources are required to start. I will not complicate it and it will be two pages or less. I will complete this plan by _____. The income model will play to my strengths described earlier in this HELP template.

4. I need resources to start my homestead business. The critical resources I need to launch are _____, _____ and _____. I will procure these resources by this date _____.

5. I, as well as those who count on me, may endure some financial hardship as I pursue this goal. I will minimize this hardship by either taking these actions to increase savings (_____,

_____), or by taking these actions to reduce expenses (_____, _____), using many of the ideas I read about in this book.

6. Once I take the leap to homesteading, I will likely run into tough times that I have yet to anticipate, so I will need a mentor or confidant to help me realize my dream. This can be a person or a community. I will rely on _____ for this.

7. If I (we) need to quit a job before transitioning to the homestead, I (we) will do so by _____.

8. I will launch my homestead business no later than _____.

9. My primary income stream will be _____ and I will get my first customer (s) by this method: _____ _____.

10. Finally, I have no intention of failing and am DETERMINED to succeed. However, I recognize that failure of any one homestead enterprise is a possibility. If I am not successful with my first choice my "fallback" income streams are _____ and _____.

My Signature   _____

Witnessed by   _____

Chapter Seven
Self-Sufficient Income

"If you don't have a dream, how are you going to make a dream come true?"
—Oscar Hammerstein

Several years ago as we prepared to transition from sprawling urban life to our rural farmstead, my wife and I were filled with excitement about growing our own food and being immersed in nature. Yet, during that period of intense change and learning we also spent many hours discussing, of all things, retirement.

At the time the idea of retirement was many years away for us, but in our "former" lives we at least understood what the plan was, so we rarely thought about it. The plan then was simply to keep working until we were 62 or so and then let a 401K or pension plan fund the rest of our life, perhaps with a little help from social security. Moving to the farm means that there may be no pension plan and for many people it means converting a 401K or other savings into hard assets such as land. Then, just as we were moving to the farm the "great recession" of 2008 hit. We witnessed the economic hardship forced onto so many people as a result of reckless lending and investments by major lending institutions and equally reckless government spending, which required government bail-outs and central banks intervention to prop up global markets. After that experience, our confidence that pension fund obligations would ever be met had eroded anyway, so we began to consider thinking of retirement planning, and homesteading, in a new way. And we are not alone in thinking this way.

HOMESTEADING AS A RETIREMENT PLAN

Consider Guy McDowell who runs a preparedness website called CanadaPrepared.com. On it, he wrote an article in 2009 that he titled Preparedness as a Retirement Plan. With Guy's permission and in his own words, here is the article in its entirety.

"You will be completely prepared to live comfortably and well with little to no income." – Guy McDowell

"**The concept of retirement is a relatively new one**. Not so long ago, when we were a more agrarian based society, few people ever retired. Their daily duties just changed. As we grew older we would take over running the farm, and then we would maybe step back and let our kids do that. Maybe we would take over maintenance of the equipment or something a little less physically demanding, but that required our experience. Maybe we would help out more inside the home. But flat-out retirement to travel south or play golf all day was the domain of the ultra rich. Even then, most tycoons were still wheeling and dealing well into their 60s and beyond.

Nowadays with retirement plans tanking and pension funds bleeding out, we may find ourselves without the ability to retire once again. However, this time, we will not have the farm to feed us and the multi-generational home to keep us occupied and close to our loved ones. If we are very fortunate we may be able to find a spot in a retirement home and sell our current homes to pay for it.

Me, I have a different plan. My plan depends on me getting prepared to take care of myself and my wife for as long as we are physically able. If my plan works we will also be able to 'retire' early. That plan is preparedness.

When you think about it if you can provide most of your own food, utilities, and medicine and your shelter is bought and paid for, how much money do you really need? Enough to pay the property taxes, run your vehicle, and take care of emergencies. Maybe you need some money for a bit of travel as well. But not as much money as two people working for more than 40 hours a week each generate.

It is not hard to imagine a household income of around $100,000 a year or about $73,000 after taxes. Now, we know a lot of people are going to have mortgage payments around $1400 a month, utilities of at least $400 a month, TV and Internet for another $200 a month, $500 for food, $400 for various insurances, $200 for gas for the vehicles…it goes on and on.

So just the cost of living consumes $3100 of your after-tax income. Yearly, that is about half of your income. If you can pay off your home, produce half of your utilities, drop the fancy TV package and step down a notch on the Internet access (that is a tough one for me) and produce half of your food, you cut that outlay to about $1100 dollars a month. At that point, one of you can effectively retire. Or, the two of you can work half as much.

So what do you do with the extra 20-30 hours a week? Do the soul-building things like work your garden, love your spouse, split some wood, read books, start a business, whatever! Now, you are working for you. And should everything go for a poop, you will be completely prepared to live comfortably and well with little to no income.

I find the thought of retiring to my homestead around the age of 50 to be a much more motivating and positive thought, than thinking of prepping to cope with disaster or the "End of the World" like stereotypical survivalists talk about. Disaster may never come, but time always marches on, and sooner or later we all need to slow down."

————————————

I agree with Guy's thinking and, in fact, we have found the life he envisages for his future to closely resemble the life we lead today. Of course we were not leading this life a decade ago when we lived "normal" lives on a small lot in suburbia, homeowner's association and all. I often found myself worrying about what would happen as we aged, which is why we took purposeful steps to increase our independence and self-reliance. As I shared in *The Accidental Farmers* I do not think we knew precisely why we were going to the country when we went... we just knew something was not right in the world we were living. Our goal was simply to begin producing more of what we needed and consuming less of what we were offered, and that transition made good financial sense. After all, consumption costs money whereas, as I have described in this book, production can save or even earn money.

Another thing I have learned is this: I do not believe someone needs a lot of money to feel "well off." If they have a lot of money, great... I suppose, unless there is a severe financial crisis, which a growing number of people expect at some point. In that event I suppose they will not be so well off after all. On the other hand if you have a spot of land on which you can raise purely pastured animals (sheep, cows, goats) you can produce more protein than you will need each year, and you can do so at ZERO cost if the animals only consume pasture. This is even more true if you have a pond and stock it with catfish, as we did, or have access to hunting ground for deer, rabbit, squirrel, etc., as we do. All "free" food for the taking and, unlike annual gardening, the food will replenish itself and require virtually zero maintenance.

Once you learn to tend a year-round garden, start seeds and save seeds, you will have no cost for seeds, and the time you now spend fighting traffic, sitting in meetings or doing your job will be spent planting, weeding, harvesting, hunting, processing, preserving and, most importantly, eating healthily! There will be plenty of downtime for pasture walks, reading, and enjoying life. In my opinion, enjoyment of a healthy life is the goal in retirement, rather than being rich. It will not take much land for you to produce enough for yourself and to generate enough income to pay taxes, etc. As I mentioned earlier, how much income you need is up to you, but regardless of the answer, this book provides numerous ways you can financially achieve a self-sufficient lifestyle.

The only caveat I would add to Guy's article is to remove the age of 50 as a target for retiring to the homestead, for why not retire much sooner if you would like? Regardless of your current age, you can think of homesteading as a retirement plan, for what you are really doing is redefining "retirement." Retirement does not mean not working; it means freedom to work as much (or as little) as you want. Some people want to work vigorously until their last day. I fear that I am in that camp. Others may want to approach work as something more of a hobby. Either approach can be realized on a homestead as long as income and expenses are aligned. The strategies in this book should prove helpful for achieving that. Again, it is not as if you will not need money, but if the goal is to have no mortgage, no utility bills thanks to alternative energy, very low food costs thanks to gardens, orchards, milk cows and livestock, no car payments, etc., how much money will you actually require? Whatever the answer to that question, the homestead rather than an employer or public pension plan can be relied upon for income, allowing you to put faith in yourself rather than others.

For example, in chapter two I described how you could simply start with a breeding group of cows to produce income for grass-fed beef. If you had the land available but no longer wanted to market the end product in your "retirement" years, you could simply let the herd breed, graze, and grow. Once they reached marketable size, you could simply sell them at the livestock market and earn thousands of dollars per year for doing very little. Add that to other passive income streams you may have created that I described in chapter three and you can see how funding a peaceful homestead retirement is very doable without the worry of whether pension obligations will be met.

PARTING WORDS OF WISDOM

As a contributing editor to Mother Earth News, Steve Maxwell wrote an excellent article for the publication in May 2012 titled "Homestead-Based Income Key to Success." In it he described a common scenario that he observes regarding new and enthusiastic homesteaders. Here is part of what Steve wrote:

"**As a homesteader, economics are much more important than I realized when I started out nearly 30 years ago.** This same oversight is one reason I regularly see new homesteaders fall into a sad scenario that often goes remarkably like this:

a) Visionary person comes to the country wanting to be part of a good and natural lifestyle.

b) Person has plans for pursuing small-scale agriculture as means of making the modest amount of money they figure is necessary for purchased essentials (i.e. a little bit of fuel, a bottle of Tylenol now and then, tools for the self-sufficient lifestyle, property taxes, etc).

c) Person underestimates the amount of money required to meet their expectations, while also overestimating the earnings they expect to come from a small-scale, agriculture-based business.

d) Economic realities (i.e. poverty) force the person to take some basic, off-homestead job "temporarily" – a job that's typically incompatible with the ideals that brought them to the country in the first place. This temporary job also takes up all the time, energy, and enthusiasm available most days.

e) Two or three or four years down the road, the visionary person runs out of enthusiasm and goes back to the city, because their life is consumed by a basic, off-homestead job and bears virtually no resemblance to the homestead lifestyle they set out to create. As noble and necessary as all legitimate occupations are, few of them mesh well with homesteading. In fact, a homestead situation is a definite drawback when you have got to travel away from it regularly to earn money."

In my experience, Steve is correct. Economics are not only important, they may be THE most important aspect of successful homesteading. New homesteaders place so much emphasis on recapturing the lost skills of gardening, food preservation, craftsmanship, and so on. Yet, as Steve indicated, new homesteaders often fall short of financial success. In the end, they learn new self-sufficiency skills but fail to become financially self-sufficient, and then return to the life they knew to be unfulfilled once again.

I do not want this to happen to you.

My intention in writing this book is to help outline some of the ways you can profitably pursue homesteading or small-scale farming without becoming a slave to the farm. After all, becoming a slave to the land is not why you want to move to the country, is it?

People who are new to farmsteading or entrepreneurial life in general are often nervous, if not downright scared, about the prospects of not having a comfortable and secure paycheck coming in each week. What I will say is that when you do make that transition and learn how to generate income for yourself that you will never again worry about whether you may get laid off, how your employer is doing, or if you will have money in retirement.

You will make the life that you want for yourself and no one will be there to deny you the pay raise if you want it, or more time off if you want that, although getting both is the ultimate triumph!

I hope this book has helped you to better understand the possible ways you can achieve financial success on the homestead. Clearly there is lots more that can be said on the topic and I encourage you to continue reading and soul-searching. There is no one right answer in terms of which business enterprise (s) you should pursue… let passion and marketability be your guide. However, if you are sitting on the fence about pursuing a life of self-sufficiency on the homestead or just staying put, let me close with one final observation from my personal experience:

MANY PEOPLE WITH URBAN JOBS HAVE TOLD ME THEY WOULD LOVE TO LEAVE THE CUBICLE TO HOMESTEAD OR FARM, BUT I HAVE NEVER HEARD A FARMER OR HOMESTEADER SAY THEY WISH THEY WERE IN A CUBICLE!

Did you find this book useful?

Please **leave a review on Amazon** and tell your followers/friends about it on Facebook, Twitter & your blog!

About the Author

While flying high over corporate America, Tim Young received a call he couldn't ignore. He shredded his business cards, said goodbye to the conveniences of urban life and become a farmsteader. Along the way Tim became an award-winning cheesemaker and Amazon best-selling author. Today he lives with his wife—the most beautiful and caring woman in the world, his delightful daughter, and a Silky Terrier named Alfie who speaks to him in condescending broken English.

Other Books by Tim Young

THE ACCIDENTAL FARMERS - AMAZON BEST SELLER! (NON-FICTION, 2011)

Praise for The Accidental Farmers

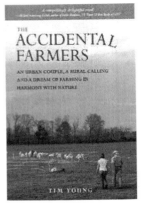

"With wit, humor and precision, Tim mesmerizes the reader as he and Liz learn how to achieve a life of harmony with the natural world. I promise you a compellingly delightful read." – **Mildred Armstrong Kalish, NY Times best-selling author of Little Heathens.**

"In a most compelling way, Tim presents that beautiful equation: healthy soil equals healthy animals equals healthy human beings." - **Sally Fallon Morell, President of the Weston A. Price Foundation**

"If you have always been attracted to rural life, this book is made for you!"- **Gene Logsdon**, author of The Contrary Farmer

The Accidental Farmers Description

The Accidental Farmers is a personal memoir of an urban couple's journey to farming and is sure to delight those interested in moving to the country or simply learning more about the struggles of sustainable farming. When Tim and Liz Young decided to leave their comfortable suburban life and become first-time farmers in rural Georgia, they embarked on a journey that would change their lives. The Accidental Farmers reveals how the couple learned that hamburgers, bacon, and eggs don't come from the supermarket but from real animals that forge emotional bonds with their human caretakers. Seeking a middle path between a meatless lifestyle and the barbarism of factory food, Tim and Liz created a sustainable oasis where rare breed animals and humans live together searching for something nearly lost by both humans and the animals… how to live naturally off the land.

Buy and read it today!

Other Books by Tim Young

POISONED SOIL - (FICTION, 2012)

Praise for Poisoned Soil

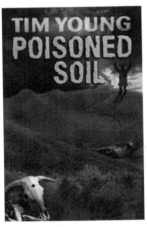

"A First Class Thriller!" - **The Kindle Book Review**

"A Cherokee curse and a hunger for success wreak havoc in this ambitious supernatural tale. The bright spots of true suspense will satisfy readers looking for a grim, inventive thriller." - **Kirkus Reviews**

"You will enjoy every minute that you're reading this book—the characters, the settings, the battles between man and nature, and, of course, that magical realism. With all these elements, this still is a thriller, a real page-turner. Moreover, it's a very original piece of literature that will leave you thinking…and wondering." – **Bookpleasures.com Review**

Poisoned Soil Description

Set in the mountains of Georgia, Poisoned Soil is a harrowing, cinematic story of greed and retribution that follows Blake Savage, a ruined football star who risks everything for a chance to make his fortune. When an egocentric restaurateur offers Blake fame and fortune to produce an illegal delicacy for his exclusive network of secret supper clubs, Blake enters a gilded world. But when the foodies take their first bites of the illicit delicacy an ancient disease resurfaces, unleashing a trail of black death. A shockingly real drama about how greed entices otherwise good people to make bad decisions, Poisoned Soil weaves a rich Appalachian tapestry and brings the natural world to life through the eyes of a remarkable family held captive on cursed Cherokee land.

Buy and read it today!

Made in the USA
Lexington, KY
21 December 2015